Just Whatever

How to Help the Spiritually Indifferent
Find Beliefs that Really Matter

Matt Nelson

Just Whatever

How to Help the Spiritually Indifferent
Find Beliefs that Really Matter

Catholic
Answers
Press

Published by Catholic Answers, Inc.
2020 Gillespie Way
El Cajon, California 92020
1-888-291-8000 orders
619-387-0042 fax
catholic.com

Printed in the United States of America

Cover design by ebooklaunch.com
Interior design by Sherry Russell

978-1-68357-077-6
978-1-68357-078-3 Kindle
978-1-68357-079-0 ePub

For Amanda, my beloved companion and a constant reflection of wisdom, goodness, and beauty in my life.

Lord, my first fruits present themselves to thee;
Yet not mine neither: for from thee they came,
And must return. Accept of them and me,
And make us strive, who shall sing best thy name.
Turn their eyes hither, who shall make a gain:
Theirs, who shall hurt themselves or me, refrain.

—George Herbert, "The Dedication"

Contents

Foreword

The advice given to Christians in the first letter of Peter has never been more relevant: "Always be ready to give an explanation to anyone who asks you for a reason for your hope, but do it with gentleness and reverence, keeping your conscience clear" (3:15–16). Our faith is the foundation of the hope that gives joy to our lives, but we do not cling to it as a private possession. We need to share it, and explain it to others.

The first Christians were engaged mainly in explaining their faith to people who had never heard of Christ, and who were perhaps curious about this new religious group in the Roman Empire. They also had to defend their faith against those who violently persecuted them; that is also the situation of Christians in many parts of the world today.

But in these days in North America and Europe, there is no overt and violent persecution. Instead, many who were raised, at least nominally, as Christians have lost their faith. Sometimes, as with the seed sown in thin soil in the Parable of the Sower (Matt. 13:1–9; Mark 4:1–20; Luke 8:4–15), their faith has never developed deep roots, and so withers away. Sometimes faith has been choked by the dominant cultural power of materialistic secularism, especially when that secularism exalts the autonomy of the ego—a vision of life far removed from the generous love modeled on that of the Trinity, which is at the heart of Christian faith. Sometimes faith has simply been taken away by the shallow but tempting arguments of advocates of atheism and agnosticism.

Believers whose faith is merely private and emotional, with no rational foundation, are particularly vulnerable. As St. John Paul II made clear, we fly to the Heavenly Father using the wings of both faith and reason. And thus many drift away from the Church, and many outside the Church are likewise convinced that Christian faith is baggage from the past, no longer relevant today. The result is often not antagonism toward faith, but simply a lack of interest in something that seems to be meaningless.

In such a situation, we need help in understanding the nature of the current phenomenon of religious indifferentism, and how to reach out effectively to those who have been affected by it. Matt Nelson's *Just Whatever: How to Help the Spiritually Indifferent Find Beliefs that Really Matter* is exactly what we need. It provides a clear analysis of the situation of religious indifferentism, and offers a way forward. It shows how to give a reason for the hope we have.

★★★

Aristotle wisely suggested that to be effective in the difficult task of communicating a valuable message of truth, it is important to build a bridge of credibility (*ethos*); to touch the heart with an approach that resonates with the whole person (*pathos*); and to communicate clearly a valuable message that is true and well argued (*logos*). All of us would do well to consider this ancient wisdom. Here Matt Nelson shows us how to be ready "to give an explanation to anyone who asks you for a reason for your hope" in a way that is not only obviously founded on a deep and vibrant faith, but which also engages us, enlightens us, and moves us to action.

First *ethos*: credibility. Matt speaks of his own journey of faith, and is clearly a person who knows personally what he is talking about. Pope Paul VI once wisely said that in matters of faith people these days will not listen to teachers but to witnesses, and only to those teachers who are also witnesses. Matt witnesses to his faith, and also clearly knows of the struggles that young people go through in these days. Sometimes it is said that the Church offers answers to questions people are not asking, but this book is based on listening to the real questions of real people.

Credibility is further enhanced because, like Thomas Aquinas in his day, Matt sincerely engages writers who do not have faith, and are eloquently antagonistic to it. He obviously has studied deeply the atheist writers who have had such a detrimental effect upon Christians whose faith is not deeply rooted. Such willingness to venture beyond the safe boundaries of Christian writings to examine honestly and thoroughly the views of those who critique the Christian faith is both courageous and essential if a writer is to be credible.

Just Whatever also touches the heart, speaking to the whole person, reflecting the *pathos* that is essential for the effective communication of truth. Though the book is obviously based on exceptional learning, it is very readable, with lots of practical examples; not dry and academic at all. Our Lord showed us the way by telling stories rather than writing dusty treatises. We must learn from this. The Church seems forever to be issuing documents, full of truth, that nobody reads. There has to be another way. I once read a book on the study of history by Barbara Tuchman. She says that every writer should have above the desk a sign that says: "Will the reader turn the page?" That is good advice. This book makes you turn the page.

Finally, if we are to give an explanation for the hope we have in a world that has tuned out the voice of faith, the credibility of the witness and the engaging style of the presentation must be matched by *logos*, by substantial, well-reasoned content. Too often we have tried to attract people by dumbing down the Faith. That is condescending, especially to young people, and it is not effective. Truth attracts. Catholic tradition attracts, for it is astonishingly rich in beauty, truth, and goodness. It is indeed a sea in which lambs may wade, and elephants may swim.

We have nothing to fear from the sterile arguments of the modern advocates of materialism, atheism, and secularism, but we do need to know how to respond to them. They are, sadly, often effective against the faith of uninstructed believers. We must meet the modern opponents of faith on their own ground, and engage them with clarity and charity, and this is certainly what happens in *Just Whatever.*

But it is even more important to experience deeply the profound richness of Catholic Christian faith. As Bishop Sheen wisely observed, to get rid of pepper in a box, the best thing is not to concentrate on the pepper but to fill the box with salt.

Reading *Just Whatever* is a delight, and a substantial intellectual feast. Certainly the various arguments against faith are analyzed and refuted but, much more than that, the book introduces the reader to the scriptural, philosophical, theological, spiritual, cultural, and literary heritage of Catholic Christianity. That in itself is a reason to treasure this book, quite apart from its astute and most useful analysis of the modern crisis of religious indifferentism.

I pray that all who read this book will not only be assisted in responding to the modern challenge of religious indifferentism, and the assaults of the dominant materialism of the secular culture, but that they will be enriched in their life of faith.

+Thomas Collins
Archbishop of Toronto

Acknowledgments

Above all I would like to thank my dear parents, Barry and Cindy Nelson, for teaching me the faith of the Church and, most of all, for modeling in themselves a life of faith, hope, and charity. Thank you to my wife, Amanda, and my sweet little girls, Anna and Emilia, for being my biggest fans and for overwhelming me with the only thing that endures in the long run: love. Thank you to my mother-in-law, Joanne Wickenheiser, for handing me my first book of Christian apologetics eight years ago.

A heartfelt thanks to Todd Aglialoro, director of publishing at Catholic Answers, who took a chance on me three years ago when he agreed to give me a shot as an author. Thank you for sticking with me and having faith in my abilities, despite my rookie ignorance and imperfections. A sincere thanks to editor Jeff Rubin for his improvements and insights into the final manuscript—this book is undoubtedly better because of you. I am deeply grateful also to my friend, His Eminence, Thomas Cardinal Collins for writing the foreword to this book and, more importantly, for his fearless defense of the true and the good in Canada.

Thank you to my friends, Jon Sorenson, Karlo Broussard, Trent Horn, Patrick Coffin, and all of the other apologists and authors at Catholic Answers, past and present, for teaching and evangelizing me long before we knew each other; and thank you for your support ever since. I will forever be indebted to you all. Thank you to Brandon Vogt for his friendship and encouragement along the way, and for his help as a reviewer of the manuscript. Finally, a special thank you to my "tribe" for taking life's big questions seriously and pursuing truth courageously by my side: Brandon Nelson, Matthew Fahlman, Kyle Banadyga, Jon Courchene, Justin Hughes, Adam Fahlman, Logan Klassen, the Lanzarini brothers, Greg Lewans, Sean Milan, Lance Rosen, Ben Turland, and Joe Zambon.

Introduction

Man no longer wishes to reflect on his relationship to God
because he himself intends to become God.

—Robert Cardinal Sarah, *God or Nothing*

One day, the great jack-of-all-literary-trades and Catholic convert G.K. Chesterton heard an acquaintance remark about someone, "That man will get on; he believes in himself." Chesterton countered, "It would be much truer to say that a man will certainly fail, because he believes in himself. Complete self-confidence is not merely a sin; complete self-confidence is a weakness." He went on to support his rebuttal by writing his classic book *Orthodoxy*, which became one of the most influential defenses of Christianity in modern times.

Ever since the beginning, there has been no belief more self-destructive for man than belief in his own self-sufficiency. Ironically, it has always been one of his most acute temptations. We often desire to be our own master. Chesterton lived in the early twentieth century; consequently, he and his contemporaries didn't have the pleasure of living with "smart" technology. The trade-off was that they had to be smart themselves. Unlike them, however, we live in an age where intellectual laziness and irreverence for truth has become too easy. We have been equipped for a sort of radical self-dependency. We can deposit a check at the snap of a smartphone (who needs a bank teller?), edit an essay with autocorrect (who needs grammar?), carry Google in our pocket (who needs memory?), and choose our own gender (who needs biology?). We depend less on the talents and authority of others than ever before. We have become the masters of our own world. Our hyper-technologized, over-individualized culture has put us on the brink of omnipotence—or so it might seem. We are still not content. "How many have succumbed to the belief that man will

17

save himself when sufficient knowledge and energy are applied to the human condition?" wonders Catholic artist and cultural commentator Michael O'Brien. "I would suggest that this intrinsic perversity now dominates the entire Western world."[1]

But a world where we are "masters" is not the real world. There is an order of being in creation, and the great majority of humanity has always believed this. Indeed, the human consensus throughout past eras has been that our place on the hierarchy of being is not at the top. Modern men, however, seem not to agree. By and large, they have rejected what Chesterton called the "democracy of the dead" and adopted the opinion that we, here and now, *are* at the top and are therefore the measure of all things—drawing their "wisdom" from Protagoras, the father of relativism. At a time when we can do and decide so much for ourselves, when the power to do all things seems at our fingertips, we may be tempted to wonder: who needs God when we can be like gods? There is something peculiarly Edenic about our modern situation.

What is religious indifferentism?

I was raised in a loving Catholic family. My dad, raised a Lutheran, joined the Church when he married my mother, a cradle Catholic. As we grew up, both made a genuine effort to pass on the Faith to me and my four younger siblings. But as I grew older I became negative and critical toward the Catholic Church. It came down to this: I wanted to live one way and the Catholic Church wanted me to live another. So I chose to go my own way, focusing on realizing my worldly ambitions. Inevitably, Catholicism drifted off my radar. By the time I had completed university I no longer accepted the traditional Christian morality and beliefs I had been taught; and I harbored a growing skepticism, particularly about the divinity of Christ and the personal nature of God. These doubts rendered all organized forms of religion, Catholicism included, increasingly irrelevant to me. Eventually tempted by agnosticism, I found myself absorbed into a pagan way of life, and my doubts about Catholicism continued to increase. I was not a vocal opponent of the Catholic Church; nor can I say that I was intellectually engaged in discovering whether God existed or not. I was, for lack of a better phrase, following my feelings which were drawing me toward an Epicurean way of life; that is, a Godless one focused on pleasure and convenience. Yet, despite my disengagement from organized religion and my growing skepticism towards the God of monotheism, I could not altogether shake my sense that there had to be more to reality than just what I could see, touch, and hear. I retained a stubborn sense of spirituality—although I was not altogether sure of what *exactly* I believed in. On some days I found deism most attractive; on other days I was more inclined towards a pantheistic, New Age spirituality. On most days I lived as though I was an atheist. But intellectually, none of these inclinations ever transformed into convictions deep enough to affect any significant commitment. At best, I could describe myself as "spiritual but not religious."

My detachment from so-called organized religion was not the result of any sort of strict intellectual groundwork. I had not contended with arguments against Catholicism, or against any other religion, and lost. I had just drifted away from commitment to Christ and his Church and grown indifferent to religious matters. Life was busy and much too stimulating to bother with such things.

My story illustrates the central psychological problem of the modern era: whereas man is by nature a creature made for both heaven and earth, he no longer knows it. He no longer cares. It is hard to say which came first, the ignorance or the indifference. It is not difficult to conclude, nonetheless, that both have arrived. Thus, for the sake of his present happiness and his future glory, man must be woken up. The urgency here is real, for as the great twentieth-century martyr St. Maximilian Kolbe assessed, "The most deadly poison of our times is indifference."

What is religious indifference? In the broadest sense it is the failure to take religious questions seriously and, as a result, the failure to give to God what is his due. So there is both an *intellectual* and a *practical* arm of religious indifference. The three main parts of this book, however, will focus more narrowly on three specific types of religious indifferentism, all of which you have likely encountered in some form.

The first type is *closed indifference*, which involves closed-mindedness toward religion. Closed indifferentists reject all religions. But although they believe all religions are untrue, closed indifferentists are not necessarily unfriendly toward religion. As the atheist philosopher Julian Baggini writes, "Atheists can be indifferent rather than hostile to religious belief. They can be more sensitive to aesthetic experience, more moral, and more attuned to natural beauty than most theists."[2]

Maybe you've encountered the atheist who couldn't care less about religion; or the deist whose god "pushed the first domino" to set time and matter into motion but, like a deadbeat father, turned his back on his creation ever since. Perhaps you have met people who think of God more as an impersonal Force than a loving Father. It should be no surprise, then, that these nontheists see religion as insignificant (*nontheist* meaning those who do not believe in a God who remains in close personal contact with his creation and who acts in the world here and now). Where the problem lies for the closed indifferentist is in his failure to reckon seriously with arguments for and against a personal God's existence.[3] For closed indifferentists, a Christian's primary evangelistic goal should be to show them that there are good reasons to believe in the existence of a personal God.

The second type of religious indifference is *open indifference*. Whereas closed indifference involves a total closed-mindedness to religion, open indifference is characterized by an extreme open-mindedness toward all religions. Open indifferentists generally hold that all religions—and religious founders—are equal. By doing so, they reduce Jesus to a non-savior or one savior among many. This is a common feature of New Age spirituality. New Age guru Deepak Chopra, for example, writes, "I want to offer the possibility that Jesus was truly, as he proclaimed, *a* savior. Not *the* savior, not *the* one and only Son of God. Rather, Jesus embodied the highest level of enlightenment [emphasis added]."[4]

Maybe you've interacted with, say, a "spiritual but not religious" college student who praises the teachings of Jesus while putting Gautama Buddha or the Dalai Lama on the same pedestal, as if *all* spiritualities lead equally to the same God. Underneath such notions commonly lie an aversion to "organized religion." To open indifferentists, there is no one religion that is truer than another. Thus, when it comes to open indifferentists, a Christian's primary evangelistic goal should be to show them that Jesus was who he claimed to be: the one God of heaven and earth.

The third type of religious indifference is *denominational indifference*. Denominational indifferentists claim that all Christian denominations are equal. The existing *doctrinal* contradictions between denominations is thereby underappreciated and waved aside as of little importance. The great Anglican convert John Cardinal Henry Newman identified this sort of indifference, already prevalent in the nineteenth century, when he wrote in *An Essay on the Development of Doctrine*, "The hypothesis, indeed, has met with wide reception in these latter times, that Christianity does not fall within the province of history—that it is to each man what each man thinks it to be, and nothing else."[5]

Perhaps you've met a self-described Christian who rejects the importance of doctrine and accordingly does not take disagreements among denominations seriously. Instead, perhaps, they assert that so long as Christians of different stripes worship the same Jesus Christ then all is well. So whether a person happens to be Roman Catholic or Southern Baptist, Greek Orthodox or Quaker, it doesn't ultimately matter—even when their doctrines clearly contradict each other. That is denominational indifference. For denominational indifferentists, a Catholic's primary evangelistic goal should be to show that there are good reasons to believe that the Catholic Church is the one Church founded by Christ as revealed in the New Testament.

So you can see that religious indifferentism is not easy to define in all its forms and complexities, and exists across a broad spectrum of religious attitudes ranging from "nothing goes" to "anything goes."[6] But underlying them all is a "*just whatever*" mentality—an apathy toward spiritual and religious truth that reflects our culture's infatuation with relativism and "tolerance," and its addiction to cheap pleasures and mindless entertainment. *If your God thing works for you*, great, the mentality goes, *but my lifestyle is working just fine without it.*

Our purpose in the pages to come, then, is to explore the problem of indifference—as well as its price. For if Catholicism *is* true, it follows that the great spiritual problem of our day is not *what* many people think about Catholicism, but that many people *don't* think about Catholicism. Indeed, all too often, deluded by logical, historical and biblical falsehoods, they only react to it without a second thought. As a result, and to their own harm, they live their lives according to a defective vision of reality.

Underlying philosophies

Let's look a little deeper at the three types of religious indifference just outlined. Closed indifferentism commonly results from an atheistic worldview—though not always. It may also arise from a deistic worldview. While deists believe in a supernatural creator of the universe, they reject the idea of a personal, loving God who is always present to his creation. So even though deists believe in a creator, deism still shares at least one key principle with atheists: there is no intelligent being greater than ourselves at work in this world. Though God is responsible for the birth—the winding up, as it were—of the universe, he is long gone. Worshipping God, according to the atheistic and deistic worldviews, is therefore absurd, because there is no God present to watch, listen, or respond. Closed religious indifference would make sense if God either did not exist or was not personal, because the absence of an attending God in this world would rule out the possibility of any divinely-imposed beliefs or obligations. It would also rule out the prospect of divine judgement. The question is, of course, whether there *are* good reasons to take the prospect of an existent personal God seriously. But let's move on and consider the fundamental philosophy underlying both the open and denominational types of indifferentism (which are probably the two most common forms of indifferentism today). That philosophy is *relativism*. Relativism is the rejection of objective, mind-independent truth in favor of one's subjective, personal opinion: therefore, all matters of truth actually come down to what is true "for you." Relativism rejects all dogma; yet it is itself dogmatic in its insistence that it is objectively true that there are no objective truths. See the problem? Relativism refutes itself—and yet *this* is the philosophy that drives much of the thinking and decision-making in our time. As a result, people are becoming less concerned about what is true than about what is convenient. The relativistic "just do it" mindset has sunk its numbing tentacles into the frontal lobe of modernity, and the result has been intellectual paralysis. It is thus no surprise why Cardinal Joseph Ratzinger (the future Pope Benedict XVI) called relativism the greatest problem of our time.[7]

Seeds of indifference

Man's sin-damaged nature also has something to do with religious indifference. One person who understood this profoundly was the physicist and mathematician Blaise Pascal, who (along with Pierre de Fermat) has been called the father of probability theory. He could also be called the father of modern Christian apologetics. Living during the seventeenth-century Enlightenment, Pascal (especially in his classic *Pensées*) offered arguments for Christianity that were particularly well-suited to a post-medieval, dechristianized world. Few Catholic thinkers have thought more deeply and written more astutely about the problem of religious indifference than he. In fact, the late Avery Cardinal Dulles goes so far as to say in his widely appreciated *A History of Apologetics*, "Few if any apologetical works [compared to the *Pensées*] have brought so many unbelievers on the way to faith."[8] Pascal's reflections begin with human nature and the fact of our wretchedness without God. We are never completely satisfied—and all the worse without a personal relationship with our Creator, to the point of being miserable. We are broken, which is why we are always chasing happiness. And yet we never quite find it in this life. We can never find rest in anything worldly.

The only antidote to our misery, Pascal concludes, is religion; that is, a relationship—an intimate *friendship*—with God. We accomplish that most readily by seeking to know and love Jesus Christ, since "there is salvation in no one else" (Acts 4:12). Only by knowing Jesus can we make sense of life and death, God and humanity. The problem, however, is that—unlike in the Middle Ages when Christianity was the cultural norm—modern man resists the antidote. "Men despise religion", writes Pascal. "They hate it, and fear it is true."[9] And it is because of this fear and loathing of religion that men turn to two distinct strategies of avoidance: *diversion* and *indifference*.

It is easy to see how diversion works. Whether in the form of pleasure-seeking, ambitious striving, or sheer busyness, we have all probably caught ourselves using this strategy to avoid some of life's hard realities. Those prone to procrastination (like myself) will especially understand how this works. But our current concern is with indifference—the result of diversion and a distinct problem in itself.

Whereas diversion involves an effort to distract oneself, indifference involves a *lack of effort* to sincerely seek a relationship with God. Pascal poses a challenge to the Church's critics: "Let them at least learn what this religion is which they are attacking before attacking it. . . . They think they have made great efforts to learn when they have spent a few hours reading some book of the Bible, and have questioned some ecclesiastic about the truths of the faith. After that they boast that they have sought without success in books and among men."[10] Life without God is absurd, thinks Pascal. How can anyone be so content with such a superficial search—or no search at all—for the divine? He contemplates the barrenness of life without God:

And how can such an argument as this occur to a reasonable man? "I do not know who put me into the world, nor what the world is, nor what I am myself. I am terribly ignorant about everything. I don't know what my body is, or my senses, or my soul, or even that part of me which thinks what I am saying, which reflects about everything and about itself, and does not know itself any better than it knows anything else. I see the terrifying spaces of the universe hemming me in, and I find myself attached to one corner of this vast expanse without knowing why I have been put in this place rather than that . . . All I know is that I must soon die, but what I know least about is this very death which I cannot evade. Just as I do not know whence I come, so I do not know whither I am going. All I can know is that when I leave this world I shall fall forever into nothingness or into the hands of a wrathful God, but I do not know which of these two states is to be my eternal lot."[11]

Pascal is rattled by man's staunch indifference toward the search for God because, as he rightly sees, how we should best live hinges above all on whether eternal happiness is truly possible. One thing is for sure: we are wretched in this life. And whether or not that wretchedness will ever give way to real, lasting happiness depends wholly on whether heaven after death really exists. "All our actions and thoughts," writes Pascal, "must follow such different paths, according to whether there is hope of eternal blessings or not."[12] And yet, man is indifferent. Sin has taken hold, and he cares nothing to remedy the effects. Sin is both the principle cause and the effect of religious indifference.

But sin is also one the key facts about life that justify religious belief. Chesterton famously observed that original sin is the only Catholic dogma that can really be proved. What he meant is that evidence of man's brokenness is everywhere: on the street, at work, in our families, in ourselves. The human experience is characterized by a constant tension between what we *want* to do and what we *ought* to do. We struggle to understand our own actions because we often *do not* do what we know we ought to.

As St. Paul put it, we do not do the good we want, but the evil we do not want is what we do (Rom. 7:15–20).

Chesterton points out that modern masters of the sciences begin all inquiry with basic facts—or what are sometimes called "first principles." They start by believing unprovable assumptions, such as that the laws of nature will be the same tomorrow as today or that the external world is real and not a *Matrix*-like hallucination. None of these assumptions can be proved; they can only be *intuited*. Just as a table cannot stand without its legs, science cannot work without such fundamental facts. First principles ground us in reality.

Well, Chesterton observed the same thing with ancient masters of religion, all of whom began with the first principle of sin or evil. All through history it has been apparent to conscientious observers that man is broken, that he is not as he ought to be; or as Christianity has it, that he is not how he once was. Until modern times "the strongest saints and the strongest skeptics alike took positive evil as the starting point of their argument."[13] For believers, evil in the world proved that something of a fracture has occurred between man and God, whereas for nonbelievers evil justified their denial of God's existence. The same data—namely, man's inclination towards evil—has served as evidence both for and against God's existence. Thus, in the past, the fact of evil *interested* both believers and nonbelievers alike. Now, in the postmodern age, the facts of sin and evil are often dismissed altogether.

Chesterton concluded that we can no longer begin with sin as our starting point for justifying religion—because in an individualistic culture like ours, where moral relativism is rampant, the idea of sin has been declared obsolete. Instead, a better starting point is sanity. Because while modern man will deny the reality and threat of sin, he will not yet deny the existence of intellectual absurdity. Men deny sin—but not, as yet, insanity, argues Chesterton. "I mean that as all thoughts and theories were once judged by whether they tended to make a man lose his soul," he writes, "so for our present purpose all modern thoughts and theories may be judged by whether they tend to make a man lose his wits."[14]

Stop the insanity!

The truth is we have been insane for a very long time—humanity, I mean. Among the hereditary effects of Adam's sin in the Garden of Eden was the darkening of the intellect, the narrowing of the mind. As a result, we see the real world less clearly; because of our rebellion against God we see as "in a mirror dimly." Much too easily we fall out of touch with reality. This failure to see what is really there and to live accordingly is, one could say, a kind of sin-induced insanity.

"Insanity is all about us," declared the great twentieth-century author and apologist Frank Sheed. "I do not mean that men individually are madmen, but they add up to a society which is not truly sane. . . . As a society ours does not see the major part of reality at all."[15] Sheed made the distinction between two basic kinds of insanity. The first involves seeing with the mind what is not really there; this is our typical notion of insanity. We think of people snared and snookered by illusion, like the man who believes he is a chicken. The second kind of insanity is an inside-out version of the first: it involves the failure to see what is really there. So, whereas the first kind sees too much, the second sees too little. As a Catholic apologist and author, Sheed was most concerned with this second kind of insanity, which is the one that immediately concerns us. For it is the failure, and often the refusal, to see what is really there that lies behind the modern problem of religious indifference.

The adjective *sane* comes from the Latin *sanus*, meaning "healthy" or "whole." Sanity refers to a healthy intellect. And since the intellect's purpose is to know—and not merely anything but the truth, the whole truth and nothing but the truth— then to be intellectually healthy is to know the difference between what is true and what is false. When we come to know more truths and believe fewer falsehoods, we grow in sanity and our existence gains a more precise trajectory. Thus, according to Sheed, "Sanity means seeing what's there and planning life accordingly."[16] It is not enough merely to *know* what is true, because one can ignore truths and act as if they were not true. A sane person allows the truth to move him toward the good; he does not disregard it. The man who downplays the dangers of cigarettes to justify his smoking habit is less sane than the man who chooses to quit for the sake of a healthier future. The panicked young man who convinces his girlfriend to abort a newly conceived "clump of cells," when deep down he knows that the embryo is much more than that, is not planning life according to what he knows to be true; rather, he has told himself an *un*truth and planned life according to *that*. The sane man lives consistently with what he knows to be true; he discovers the truth, ponders it, and harmonizes his life with reality. Contrarily, "to act without full vision [of reality] is a formula for chaos."[17]

It is a hard fact that reality often turns out to be the opposite of what we want. Other times it proves to be the opposite of what we think. Still other times it turns out to be beyond our understanding. Indeed, there are some aspects of reality that can never be fully understood by the natural light of reason. But true sanity does not entail fully grasping the inscrutable, the mysterious. Rather, it involves a recognition that there are higher truths we cannot attain to on our own. Sheed reminds us:

> Sanity, remember, does not mean living in the same world as everybody else; it means living in the real world. But some of the most important elements in the real world can be known only by the revelation of God, which it is theology's business to study. Lacking this knowledge, the mind must live a half-blind life, trying to cope with a reality most of which it does not know is there. This is a wretched state for an immortal spirit, and pretty certain to lead to disaster.[18]

This last sentence gets to the heart of the problem. Because if we have immortal souls that live after bodily death, then we must face the possibility that what we choose to believe and how we choose to live may have eternal consequences.

The problem with religious indifference is that it entails the rejection of certain realities that have great significance, not just in this life but also in the next. To be indifferent to God is to be indifferent not only to one's Creator, but to the very ground of existence, meaning, and morality. To be indifferent to Jesus Christ is not only to be impartial to history's most influential human being, but to the divine Savior who determines one's eternal destiny. To be indifferent toward the Catholic Church is not only to be indifferent toward the Church defended by the likes of Irenaeus, Athanasius, and Augustine, but toward the sacraments of grace instituted by Christ.[19] The religious indifferentist does not have a full vision of reality. He is like the man who is blind in one eye and color-blind in the other.

What I want to get across is that indifference to Catholicism, to whatever degree, has its costs. Too many people underestimate these costs—or don't estimate them at all. I am *not* saying that sanity belongs to Catholics alone. Such a claim would make *me* insane. We are all in the struggle for a flawless view of reality. Nobody understood this better than Frank Sheed, who offered this reflection at the outset of *Theology and Sanity*:

> As to sanity, nothing has happened to diminish either my devotion to it or my awareness of its difficulty. For me it is still a distant hope and striving. It would be wonderful to die sane.[20]

The anatomy of doubt

Indifferentism breeds doubt and skepticism. But I do not wish to demonize every doubter and skeptic. In fact, an important distinction can be made between "good" doubt and "bad" doubt.

We are all prone to doubt. Let's not pretend that belief in the supernatural is always a walk in the park. Most Christians, if they are being honest, will admit that they have encountered difficulties along the path of faith and have been tempted, especially in the face of suffering and evil, to reconsider their convictions. Not even the saints have been exempt. St. Teresa of Calcutta, for example, experienced powerful temptations to religious doubt. In a letter to her confessor she wrote, "Do not think that my spiritual life is strewn with roses—that is the flower which I hardly ever find on my way. Quite the contrary, I have more often as my companion 'darkness.'"[21] How, we might wonder, can a true saint experience such temptations? But our difficulty in sensing the presence of God is a symptom of sin, and we have all been broken by sin—even the saints!

In fact, *doubt* in the sense of "difficulty" (such as what St. Teresa experienced) presupposes belief, or the acceptance of a truth based on the authority of another. And wherever belief is, doubt often follows. Why? Because we are keenly aware of our human fallibility. We know we can (and do) get some things wrong, and we know that others do too. Which can lead us to fear being wrong in our religious convictions. "Perhaps I am wrong," we might think. "Perhaps it *isn't* true." And it is not only believers who must face this fear, but unbelievers too. Even the most hardened atheist must eventually admit uncertainty about what he *cannot* see. Perhaps it *is* true," he may privately and painfully wonder. The point is that doubt can be understood as a natural possibility that arises from authentic belief. Thus, Cardinal Ratzinger wrote in his *Introduction to Christianity*:

> Both the believer and the unbeliever share, each in his own way, doubt *and* belief if they do not hide from themselves and from the truth of their being. Neither can quite escape either doubt or belief; for the one, faith is present *against* doubt; for the other, *through* doubt and in the *form* of doubt.[22]

Can doubt therefore be good? Since it seems to be a human predilection, the answer would appear to be yes, insofar as a person's doubt is not of their own fault. There appear to be three causes of unbelief: time, indifference, and contempt. For those who seek God with all their heart, an encounter with God in a real and transformative way is only a matter of time. But for indifferentists or antitheists, unbelief is a chosen and accepted state of mind and heart. The Catholic Church teaches that atheism is a sin against the virtue of religion because, according to Scripture, God has adequately revealed himself in nature.[23] This is confirmed by pagan philosophers such as Plato and Aristotle, who began with no religious premises but argued to the existence of God from what they observed in the natural world before their eyes. So, doubt in the most absolute sense—atheism, in other words—is without excuse.

But *temptation* to doubt—like any temptation we experience passively—is not in itself to be condemned. Indeed, insofar as it stimulates us to contemplate further the mysteries of religion and grow in moral character, a trial of faith may refine and strengthen our religious conviction and thus be considered a *good*. Fr. Dwight Longenecker suggests that we "experience trials in the faith for three reasons: to strengthen us, to clarify our beliefs, and to help us proclaim the gospel."[24] Indeed, doubt compels us to examine our deepest convictions about reality. And as Socrates said, only the examined life is worth living. Therefore, doubt makes life interesting, because it forces us to *think* about reality; it awakens the mind and restores the will; it compels us to make new or renewed decisions about where we are going in life. G.K. Chesterton, a convert from agnosticism, understood the potential value of doubt when he remarked, "Man must have just enough faith in himself to have adventures, and just enough doubt of himself to enjoy them."[25]

A good illustration of the tension between doubt and belief can be found in J.R.R. Tolkien's *Lord of the Rings,* when Frodo vows before the Council of Elrond, "I will take the ring, though I do not know the way." It is clear that Frodo doesn't know how he is going to pull it off. It is also clear that his will is fixed: he *will* march forward despite the thousand difficulties clamoring in his imagination. Frodo is allowing his mind and will to lead him, rather than his emotional apprehensions. He follows his deeper sense of duty, or what we might call his "feelings beneath his feelings." What is missing in the hearts of indifferentists is this will to believe that St. Teresa of Calcutta and Venerable Frodo of Bag End possessed. This is not to say that doubters should "fake it till they make it"; rather, they should will to know the truth and follow it to its logical conclusions. *The opposite of an indifferentist is a sincere seeker, not necessarily a believer.* Doubt that results from indifferentism is primarily a problem of the will; and from a lazy will follows a lazy intellect.

What if Catholicism is true?

I fear that many arguments in favor of the claims of Catholicism have not been tried and found wanting; they have been found inconvenient and left ignored. And yet this is a curious thing, since every human being desires the truth; that is, they wish to *conform their minds to reality* in order to live in the real world. No one wakes up in the morning hoping to be on the receiving end of lies and deceptions. No one loves to be lied to. Nobody craves delusion. We naturally prefer the real and the true to the fake and the false. No woman seeks a lying husband, and no employer is looking for dishonest employees. If there are objectively binding traffic laws, then naturally we want to know what they are. (Imagine a world where "your traffic laws are your traffic laws, and mine are mine.")

By knowing how things really are, we can act toward them *as* they really are. We desire truth because we desire to live in the real world. We are, after all, what Aristotle called "rational animals." Our desire for truth stems from our desire to act rationally. Therefore, the desire for truth is a deeply *human* thing. In the words of philosopher Robert Sokolowski, the desire for truth (or what he calls *veracity*) "is very deep in us, more basic than any particular desire or emotion. . . . We are made human by it, and it is there in us to be developed well or badly."[26] As humans we cannot choose whether or not to desire truth; that is instinctual to us. We can, on the other hand, choose whether to act on—and cultivate—that desire.

St. Augustine understood the human person's innate desire to know the truth of things. In his *Confessions* he reflected that he had "met many who wanted to deceive, but none who wanted to be deceived".[27] And can't we confirm this by looking inside ourselves? Our interior experience confirms that, all in all, we want the whole truth and nothing but the truth. Why? Because truth leads to order; and as Augustine observed in *The City of God*, peace is the tranquility of order. So truth leads to order, order to peace, and peace ultimately to happiness. In other words: *truth fosters happiness.* So if happiness matters, then truth matters; and we have no reason to doubt that happiness matters to all people. Aristotle, reflecting on "the highest of all goods achievable by action" observed that "the general run of men . . . say that it is happiness, and identify living well and faring well with being happy."[28] But you cannot live well and fare well if you are not planning and living out your life in accordance with reality. Insanity is not the way to real, lasting happiness.

What then if Catholicism *is* true? What if being a devout believer really can lead to greater sanity and greater happiness—even the *greatest* sanity and happiness? The Catholic faith does not just offer a more complete vision of reality. The central promise of the Catholic faith is the everlasting fulfillment of all our desires through union with God. God promises—on the Catholic view—to prepare us in this life for the fulfilment of all our desires in the next. In other words, Catholicism offers a way—*the* Way—to everlasting happiness. For God promises to fill and complete us, to make us *like him*—or what St. Peter called "partakers of the divine nature" (2 Pet. 1:4). In other words, God wants to bring to fulfillment our being made "in the image and likeness of God," and he wants to do it in the fullest sense. And that is why we can agree with Pascal that to be saved by God and enter into eternal life in Christ is to "win everything."[29]

Some may reel at such seemingly incredible claims, thinking it rather arrogant for the Catholic Church to position itself as the "pillar and foundation of truth," the *one* religion through which people can best realize happiness in this life and total fulfillment in the next. What a claim! Karl Marx was right when he called religion the "opium" of the people; especially if by religion he was thinking especially of Catholicism. This claim I am making is nothing new. The invitation to repent and believe in the Good News—and to reap its glorious fruits—has been on offer for a very long time. Catholicism is not some novel or fringe worldview. It is the most prevalent religion in the world, even 2,000 years since it burst onto the scene. And to a wide swath of humanity, it has always had a profound appeal; it has been found believable by men and women, educated and uneducated, in every age and culture. Many have even considered it worth dying for. The point: Catholicism and its radical claims deserve, at the very least, serious intellectual engagement from even the most skeptical or indifferent.

PART I

Why Worship God?

There are more things in heaven and earth, Horatio,
Than are dreamt of in your philosophy.

—William Shakespeare, *Hamlet*

1

What Kind of Universe Do We Live In?

When I was twelve years old I was in a serious automobile accident. It was early December, and seven of us were packed in a minivan. We were on our way to play a hockey game just thirty minutes away. Several minutes into the trip I undid my seatbelt to participate in the rambunctiousness in the back seat. Moments later we hit ice. The van lost control and nose-dived into a steep ditch, throwing me out of my seat, through a window, and into the path of the rolling mass of steel and rubber. Two of my friends were also thrown from the van. When I regained consciousness, I found myself underneath the upside-down minivan.

First responders were quickly on the scene and, after spending an hour pinned under the wreckage, I was finally pulled free and rushed to the hospital. Two of us were hospitalized overnight. I had sustained a concussion, hypothermia, frostbite, and various soft-tissue injuries—but the next day we were both released from the hospital. In fact, all seven of us essentially walked away from that accident. As you can imagine, this near-tragedy was the talk of our small prairie town for many days afterward. It seemed like no one talked about the accident without using spiritually charged words like "miracle" and "guardian angel," and I was constantly told that "Someone" must have been watching over me.

It should be no surprise that this close brush with death was, for me, a jarring wake-up call. It compelled me to think far beyond my pre-accident twelve-year-old cares. Thus began my sincere contemplation of those deep existential questions which, at some point in life, haunt every human creature: *Why am I here? Where am I going? How do I get there? What's the meaning of all this?*

For me, these questions had profound religious implications. As a child I had always taken God's existence, and his personal interest in *me*, for granted. But suddenly I found myself wondering whether some heavenly being *really* prevented my demise that day. In the motion picture of my imagination it was easy to imagine the hand of God reaching down and breaking my fall—but it was also easy to imagine elves making toy trains in Santa's workshop. If the elves were fantasy rather than reality, how could I be sure that God's "saving hand" was not also fantasy? I found myself in a state of solemn curiosity.

Had some supernatural person really been watching over me—or was it just a big fluke? Could an all-powerful creator of the universe really be *that* interested in my speck of a life? If I was ever going to make sense of my place and purpose in the drama of existence, I needed to find good answers to these questions.

Making God

A delusional sense of self-sufficiency has stifled much of the religious impulse of modern humanity. Our ability to do and decide things on our own has never been more enabled, thanks particularly to cutting-edge "smart" technology and the "live and let live" spirit of the age. For this reason, the concepts of religion and doctrinal authority have become off-putting, because they threaten to displace man from his relativistic throne of power. Some men make themselves enemies of religion. Many more just divert their attention from life's fundamental questions by restlessly absorbing themselves in worldly striving, self-enhancement, or other fast-fleeting vanities. Yet the religious impulse of humanity persists, and even many people who are indifferent or hostile toward organized religion still acknowledge some form of spiritual reality, some idea of the divine, however obscure and self-tailored that might be. Everyone, it seems, desires to worship *something*; that is, to find something that gives their life meaning in a more absolute way, something to explain their existence and to answer the other big questions of life. For many atheists, for instance, "Science" or "Evolution" have come to play such a role, being posited as that almighty entity, worthy of reverence and exaltation, which in and of itself can provide the answers to all of life's biggest questions. Even "atheist churches" have become a modern thing, where non-believers congregate—often on Sunday—for atheistic sermons, contemplation, and hymns (Google it!). Whether their primary intention is to congregate out of mockery, or for a genuine celebration of their unbelief, or both, they betray an *innate* human desire to acknowledge—as a community of believers—that in which they all believe. As Thomas Merton, a Catholic convert and Trappist monk (not to mention one of the greatest spiritual writers of the twentieth century), observed in his modern classic *The Seven Storey Mountain*:

> It is a law of man's nature, written into his very essence, and just as much a part of him as his desire to build houses and cultivate the land and marry and have children and read books and sing songs, that he should want to stand together with other men in order to acknowledge their common dependence on God, their Father and Creator. In fact this desire is much more fundamental than any other purely physical necessity.[30]

But man is not just made by God and for God. He is also created in God's image and likeness. He has a mind. He possesses free will. He can act intentionally and rationally. Yet despite this God-like nature, we have a disordered tendency to make God in *our* own image, as an easy alternative to becoming more like him. Consider how we are becoming more and more impersonal in our communication with others, via text messaging, email, and social media. Person-to-person, face-to-face contact is thus at an all-time low. Absorbed in our screens, we exert more energy "friending" and trying to be "followed" than spending time—slow time—building real, lasting friendships. We are preoccupied with the "useful," trying to get more done in less time—so that we can do even more. The truth is we *should* be getting more done in less time, given the gadgets and productivity apps we have at our fingertips. We *should* be spending more time with our families and loved ones, building friendships and basking in the restorative joy of leisure. But leisure is an all-but-forgotten pleasure. And so is friendship in many respects—at least the kind of friendship, *philia*, that C.S. Lewis defends in *The Four Loves*. "Friendship is unnecessary, like philosophy, like art, like the universe itself (for God did not need to create)," he writes. "It has no survival value; rather it is one of those things that gives value to survival."[31] Many of the best things in life are pure gift. And many of us, in our obsessive need for success and our addiction to noise and busyness, have thrown away some of the best things in life—and for what end? We could all benefit from contemplating Aristotle's profound statement that "without friends no one would choose to live, though he had all other goods."[32]

On technological autopilot, we have become increasingly impersonal and restlessly pragmatic—and have accordingly made God in our image. Perhaps that is why God, for many, has also become an impersonal but *useful* deity, and why the New Age cult of spirituality has become such a fad. The magisterial reflection on the New Age, *Jesus Christ the Bearer of the Water of Life*, describes well that popular approach to spirituality:

> There is talk of God, but it is not a personal God; the God of which *New Age* speaks is neither personal nor transcendent. Nor is it the Creator and sustainer of the universe, but an "impersonal energy" immanent in the world, with which it forms a "cosmic unity."[33]

This God, although impersonal and thus lacking in intelligence and free will, is nonetheless a divinity whose providence can be manifested via the so-called *law of attraction*. The gist of this New Age law: think and you shall receive. "The law of attraction is that our thinking creates and brings to us whatever we think about," says Louise Hay, one of Oprah Winfrey's esteemed self-help gurus. "It's as though every time we think a thought, every time we speak a word, the universe is listening and responding to us."[34]

Now to be sure, there is much to be said about positive thinking and visualization. Especially in my athletic endeavors, I myself have utilized these psychological exercises with notable effect. But the notion of a *responsive* universe that somehow becomes *aware* of our desires and *provides* accordingly sounds awfully personal; and yet this God—this deified Universe the New Agers avow—asks nothing of us, enforces no code of ethics, requires no worship, commands nothing. It is a most convenient deity. But not only is such a being the farthest thing from what we mean by "God" in the classical Christian tradition, neither is it the sort of God that could stand up to any serious intellectual inquiry.

Nonetheless, we can deduce some valuable insights into the human condition from all the enthusiasm about New Age spirituality. Those who trust in "the Universe" clearly want there to be something *like* God out there; they just want it to be something *other* than God. But they instinctively want to rely on something greater than themselves and other humans. They know their human weaknesses and limitations and want to be able to place their trust in a divine provider—just not God. They do not want a *relationship* with God. They do not want religion. What they want is a God who helps them get things done—and then stays out of the way.

Then there are the rest of us, those who still find satisfaction and solace in "organized" religion. The world is a great mix, as it always has been, of religious, half-religious, and nonreligious; of creeds, confessions, and denials. The question is, does anyone have it right—as in *completely* right? Is there one true religion? Politically incorrect though it may be, my answer of course is yes: I believe that the one true religion is Catholicism, founded by the one true God. It is the meeting place of all the most important truths of reality. Of course, such a statement demands a reasonable defense. And that is what we will try to give in the pages to come.

What kind of universe do we live in?

All religious thinking begins with the question of God himself, as the very ground of religion and reality. It is one thing to know whether God exists; it is another thing to know what *kind* of God exists. The kind of supreme being behind creation will have a direct bearing on what kind of universe we live in, and on how we live in that universe. Thus, neither the question of God's existence nor that of his nature is expendable in the pursuit of complete sanity. Indeed, if a *personal* deity exists, then sane living begins with accepting that fundamental truth. So if we want to live in the real world, we must consider with all seriousness the possibility that a God exists who desires and deserves our love and obedience.

Traditionally, taking the "God question" seriously has been a given. Man has always entertained the possibility that a supreme being exists who deliberates and acts intentionally in the world. Of course, there have always been skeptics too, offering non-spiritual explanations for man's incurably religious nature.

Along with the question of God's existence, there has always been the question of whether or not the universe requires a creator. There are two opposing views. First is the *materialist* view, common among critics of religion. Materialists believe that reality consists only of material objects, processes, and properties, which operate according to physical laws;[35] in other words, the only reality is physical or *material* reality. Spiritual reality is ruled out. A corollary of this view is that because nothing spiritual exists, religion is absurd. But the implications of materialism go far beyond unbelief. Molecular biologist and materialist Francis Crick expounds on the far-reaching consequences of a matter-only universe:

> You, your joys and your sorrows, your memories and ambitions, your sense of personal identity and free will, are in fact no more than the behaviour of a vast assembly of nerve cells and their associated molecules.[36]

More on this shortly.

At the other end of the spectrum is the religious or *theistic* view of the universe, which understands physical reality to be something brought into existence by a supernatural being who not only creates but takes an active interest in his creation after the fact. To theists, the physical universe is only a part of the story; there is spiritual reality as well. And since this includes man's immortal soul, humanity is believed to be destined for something more than mere natural flourishing: God has endowed man with a purpose that goes far beyond material success or emotional contentment. Man is made for more than this present life can offer.

Most people today, however, have taken the anomalous middle ground between the materialist and theistic views. They seem to want the best of both worlds. Such people are often described as "spiritual but not religious." Religion, in this view, is something like ice cream: if you don't like it, then don't have it; but if you do like it, go for it. And there are many different brands and flavors to choose from, none of which is objectively "better" than any other. It's all a matter of personal preference.

As we have already observed, the "spiritual but not religious" are often willing to admit the existence of something like God who is behind the origin and evolution of the universe. To fully grasp this point, consider how the following New Age blogger views reality, and notice her admission at the end:

> You, me, the trees, the cat, the rocks, the stars, other planets, the Universe itself. We are *all* connected. All . . . One. We are all a part of a vast energy field that connects and permeates everything (which sounds an awful lot like the Force, from *Star Wars*, doesn't it?).[37]

There is certainly something practical and unimposing about this view. It serves as a good example of what many today have adopted as their divinity: something (rather than someone) that resembles a Force more than a Father. Indeed, the "spiritual but not religious" often hold ideas of God that are so devoid of concrete definition, so lacking in dogmatic clarity, that one can't be certain where on the spectrum between deism and pantheism they actually fit. One thing *is* for certain, however: this sort of deity does not demand obedience or worship. It is not an all-powerful person, but an impersonal power. We shall call this "spiritual but not religious" view the *nontheistic* view.

In the modern spiritual landscape, the nontheistic view of the universe is dominant. Why? What's so attractive about an obscure, impersonal God? One possible answer is that it allows a person to satisfy his natural religious impulse without the annoyance of moral or doctrinal obligations; therefore, one can "live and let live" in a world of wonder without any agitation of conscience—at least in theory. C.S. Lewis describes the appeal of the modern nontheistic view (which, I think he is correct in saying, is espoused too often out of carefree convenience rather than careful intellectual deliberation):

> When you are feeling fit and the sun is shining and you do not want to believe that the whole universe is a mere mechanical dance of atoms, it is nice to be able to think of this great mysterious Force rolling on through the centuries and carrying you on its crest. If, on the other hand, you want to do something rather shabby, the Life-Force, being only a blind force, with no morals and no mind, will never interfere with you like the troublesome God we learned about when we were children.[38]

Lewis nails it here. After relating it to my own experience, I can think of no better description of the psychology behind the "spiritual but not religious" worldview. Indeed, it seems that most nontheists do not want to go so far as full-blown skepticism. They are not wholly opposed to the idea of a spiritual reality; they're just opposed to a God who makes moral and religious demands. They want spirit without religion, providence without prayer, recreation without responsibility. But at what cost?

The absurd consequences of materialism

I wonder how often those who deny the existence of God and spiritual reality think about the logical consequences of their unbelief. Many have probably heard of the gloomy existential and moral consequences of atheism—they just have not reckoned seriously with them.

The modern bent toward materialism can largely be blamed on the seventeenth-century Enlightenment, whose leading thinkers included Voltaire, René Descartes, John Locke, David Hume, and Immanuel Kant. The Enlightenment was a sort of reactionary movement, a response to the scandal of religious violence and ecclesiastical corruption. It was also inspired by the Scientific Revolution: Voltaire, Hume, Kant, and company all crowded upon the shoulders of Sir Isaac Newton—the scientific hero of the seventeenth century—whose work, especially his 1687 *Principia*, ushered in a new cosmology. In light of Newton's mathematical physics, religious authority and tradition was deemed worthless, and skepticism greeted anything that could not be observed or measured—spiritual things, that is.

The Enlightenment thinkers ridiculed religious "superstition," or what they thought was belief in the absence of proof, while they praised the precision and certainty of scientific knowledge. The irony is that science itself cannot operate without its own unprovable assumptions. The skeptical philosopher David Hume—a very influential Enlightenment figure, by the way—saw this: he pointed out that inductive reasoning, or reasoning that assumes the future will resemble the past (e.g., the sun will rise tomorrow as it did today), is not grounded in anything certain. We cannot yet observe tomorrow. We don't *know* that the laws of nature will be the same tomorrow. We can only assume—then wait and see. Also, scientists put their faith in sense perception—but how can they—or anyone for that matter—know *for certain* that the world outside their mind is real? How do we know we are not now dreaming or hallucinating? How do we *know* we are not hooked up to the Matrix? Hume reflected on our credulity toward the world outside of ourselves:

It seems evident, that men are carried, by a natural instinct or prepossession, to repose faith in their senses; and that, without any reasoning, or even almost before the use of reason, we always suppose an external universe.[39]

We always suppose that the external world is real—but without reason. We just intuitively *sense* it. In fact, even reason itself is something that we rely on without any decisive evidence to validate it. To justify our belief in our reason, we have to use our reason! There is no noncircular way to defend the reliability of our minds. Hume saw this too. The bottom line is this: believers and unbelievers alike share at least *some* ungrounded beliefs about the world. As philosopher Mitch Stokes affirms:

No two of us have entirely different beliefs. We share a host of them, and the game's rules depend on such beliefs. . . . Hume was right: there are no noncircular arguments for the reliability of the senses or reason (or memory, or any of our other cognitive tools).[40]

Of course, there are plenty of beliefs that theists and non-theists would not share. And there is perhaps no greater divide than that between theists and materialists. Indeed, the costs of the materialist worldview are sobering, because it spells the destruction of many things in common experience we usually take for granted to be real. Some atheist philosophers are consistent enough to admit this; one such academic is Alexander Rosenberg of Duke University. Consider his admissions regarding what he calls "life's persistent questions" in his book *The Atheist's Guide to Reality: Enjoying Life Without Illusions*:

Is there a God? No.
What is the nature of reality? What physics says it is.
What is the purpose of the universe? There is none.
What is the meaning of life? Ditto.
Why am I here? Just dumb luck.

Does prayer work? Of course not.

Is there a soul? Is it immortal? Are you kidding?

Is there free will? Not a chance!

What happens when we die? Everything pretty much goes on as before, except us.

What is the difference between right and wrong, good and bad? There is no moral difference between them.

Why should I be moral? Because it makes you feel better than being immoral.

Is abortion, euthanasia, suicide, paying taxes, foreign aid, or anything else you don't like forbidden, permissible, or sometimes obligatory? Anything Goes.[41]

Clearly, if Rosenberg and his fellow materialists are right about the kind of universe we live in, then the world is *not* as we know it, and things about ourselves we take for granted—such as the freedom to choose our actions—are in fact nothing more than consoling illusions. And if so, then biologist Anthony Cashmore is right when he writes, "The reality is, not only do we have no more free will than a fly or a bacterium, in actuality we have no more free will than a bowl of sugar. As living systems we are nothing more than a bag of chemicals."[42] Indeed, in the materialist view, our universe is nothing but a vast field of colliding matter and empty space, full of purposeless evolutions, accidents, and illusions; and because, as scientists tell us, the universe is "winding down," both man and the universe are headed toward oblivion. As the Nobel Prize–winning physicist Steven Weinberg observes, "The more the universe seems comprehensible, the more it also seems pointless."[43] With no purpose to life except what we invent for ourselves, with no hope of life after death, and with all our greatest achievements ultimately without meaning or effect, one is left with little else than the "nausea" of existence that Jean-Paul Sartre wrote about. If God does not exist, then this meaningless existence we call our life is as good as it gets.

From this follows the question of whether life is worth living. Sartre's existentialist ally Albert Camus reflected deeply on the consequences of life without God and came to the staggering conclusion in his literary essay *The Myth of Sisyphus* that "there is only one really serious philosophical problem and that is suicide. Deciding whether or not life is worth living is to answer the fundamental question in philosophy. All other questions follow from that." Camus understood that if God does not exist and our existence is a random accident headed for nowhere, then whether life is worth living is a question for which there is no true answer. Perhaps no modern theist has argued more persuasively for the pointlessness of life without God than Christian philosopher William Lane Craig. In his essay "The Absurdity of Life Without God," he sums up the materialist's dilemma succinctly:

> If there is no God, then man and the universe are doomed. Like prisoners condemned to death, we await our unavoidable execution. There is no God, and there is no immortality. And what is the consequence of this? It means that life itself is absurd . . . without ultimate significance, value, or purpose.[44]

What would all of this mean for religion? Well, as Rosenberg admits, the materialist's world would render prayer useless, free will illusory, immortal souls nonexistent, moral truths groundless, life meaningless, and every person destined for the eternal abyss of nothingness—so religion would be one of the greatest absurdities of all.

Yet surely, in the final analysis, our lived experience tells us that things are not as materialists insist they are. Indeed, our intuitive sense of reality reels at such suggestions. Rosenberg makes the claim that "science—especially physics and biology—reveals that reality is completely different from what most people think. . . . Science reveals that reality is stranger than even many atheists recognize." To be sure, modern scientific discoveries—such as the wave-particle duality and that we are made up of over 99 percent empty space—have revealed that reality *is* much stranger than most of us think; but none of these discoveries has done (nor could do) anything to undermine belief in free will, morality, meaning, or purpose. Science simply is not in the business of addressing such things. The nonreality of such nonphysical things follows only as a *philosophical* conclusion from atheism—not a scientific conclusion from physics. In sum: there are more things in heaven and earth than are dreamt of in the materialist philosophy. This, most men have always believed. Indeed, the stark contrast of the materialist's *theoretical* world with the real world *as humans have always experienced it* is the most obvious reason why the matter-only view of reality should be rejected.

2

The Pointlessness of Life Without God

Another of my favorite parts of *The Lord of the Rings* is when Frodo laments, to the wizard Gandalf, his inherited duty as ring-bearer. He receives wise consolation in response. Unforeseen circumstances have placed him on an uncomfortable path—a dangerous *quest* upon which the future of Middle Earth depends; as the evil threat of Sauron grows, Frodo openly admits, "I wish it need not have happened in my time." Gandalf replies, "So do I, and so do all who live to see such times. But that is not for them to decide. All we have to decide is what to do with the time that is given to us."[45] He then reassures the little hobbit that there is something even beyond the forces of evil that is at work in the world. "I can put it no plainer," says Gandalf, "than by saying that Bilbo was *meant* to find the Ring, and not by its maker. In which case you also were *meant* to have it. And that may be an encouraging thought."[46]

Gandalf tells Frodo that he is meant to be the ring-bearer, implying there is a mind—and therefore a *reason*—behind it all. Don't we often tell ourselves this too? Especially in periods of pain, puzzlement, disappointment, or sorrow, how often have we said (or heard) phrases like "it was meant to be" or "things happen for a reason"? Most of us reject the notion that life consists of nothing but random events and pointless endings. The question "What is the meaning of life?" engages all of us, even those who would answer that it has none.

Many people *feel* like they exist for a reason. But it is hard to see how any notion of objective meaning or purpose could have any grounding in reality if God takes no interest in the world—or does not exist. We have already seen that if materialism is true then life is pointless. This isn't exactly controversial, for theists *or* materialists. Professor Rosenberg, as you'll recall, answered his "life's persistent questions" in this way:

Is there a God? No.
What is the nature of reality? What physics says it is.
What is the purpose of the universe? There is none.
What is the meaning of life? Ditto.
Why am I here? Just dumb luck.

"Given what we know about the sciences," writes Rosenberg, "the answers are all pretty obvious." That statement, however, is highly dubious. Theists would be quick to remind Professor Rosenberg that science can say nothing—neither for or against—regarding the meaning or purpose of life, since these are metaphysical matters (that is, *beyond* physics). Questions about the immaterial world must be left to disciplines like philosophy and theology. Indeed, science can speak about the meaning of life to us no easier than literary criticism can explain $E = mc^2$. Religious people are not the only ones to recognize science's inability to address philosophical questions: many nonbelievers have criticized those who claim otherwise. One such critic is atheist biologist Richard Lewontin, who writes:

> Our willingness to accept scientific claims that are against common sense is the key to an understanding of the real struggle between science and the supernatural. We take the side of science in spite of the patent absurdity of some of its constructs, in spite of its failure to fulfill many of its extravagant promises of health and life, in spite of the tolerance of the scientific community for unsubstantiated just-so stories, because we have a prior commitment, a commitment to materialism.[47]

Rosenberg wants to claim that the answers to all of life's most persistent questions boils down to the answers given to us (either now or in the future) by physics. Physics, he contends, is the most fundamental kind of knowledge about reality. First, this claim *itself* is not one that physics can authenticate. Second, however, as even the famous twentieth-century atheist philosopher Bertrand Russell admits, there are obvious limitations to physics when it comes to providing knowledge about the world before our eyes:

> It is not always realized how exceedingly abstract is the information that theoretical physics has to give. It lays down certain fundamental equations which enable it to deal with the logical structure of events, while leaving it completely unknown what is the intrinsic character of the events that have the structure . . . as to what it is that changes, and what it changes from and to—as to this physics is silent.[48]

For a concrete view of reality, then, we need more than physics. We need more than the physical sciences. For, only by going beyond what science tells us can we put flesh on the bones of the real world, as it were, and view reality—even physical reality—in all its concreteness.

Because of their prior commitment to materialism, many nonbelievers read their skeptical opinions about the spiritual world *into* scientific conclusions, rather than *out of* philosophical principles. Materialists thus suffer from what Chesterton called "the combination of an expansive and exhaustive reason with a contracted common sense."[49] The trouble with materialists is not that they are scientific, but that they are *only* scientific. They accept *only* what they can know through observation and measurement, preventing them from taking seriously even the possibility of immaterial realities such as free will, moral laws, angels, demons, and God himself. Immortality is deemed an absurdity. Everything comes from atoms, and to atoms all shall return. Man himself is just a bag of decomposing chemicals.

No purpose in a Godless world

According to the atheist worldview, there is no good reason to believe in any sort of ultimate plan or purpose for human existence. We exist by chance. Our ultimate destiny is nothingness.

Bertrand Russell put it eloquently in his somber 1903 reflection, "A Free Man's Worship":

> That Man is the product of causes that had no prevision of the end they were achieving; that his origin, his growth, his hopes and fears, his loves and his beliefs, are but the outcome of accidental collocations of atoms; that no fire, no heroism, no intensity of thought and feeling, can preserve individual life beyond the grave . . . only within the scaffolding of these truths, only on the firm foundation of unyielding despair, can the soul's habitation henceforth be safely built.

The materialist's universe precludes objective human purpose. By objective purpose I mean a reason for being that is a *fact* whether one knows it—or likes it—or not. But if there exists no transcendent purpose-giver, then either "unyielding despair" or consoling fictions are all we have to build our lives on. If there is no purpose-giver, then there is no *reason* to be alive. If life is pointless, then as Macbeth put it:

> Life's but a walking shadow, a poor player
> That struts and frets his hour upon the stage
> And then is heard no more: it is a tale
> Told by an idiot, full of sound and fury,
> Signifying nothing.[50]

We can dream up a subjective purpose for ourselves. Or we can submit to the evolutionary naturalist's position that our sole purpose is to (randomly) propagate DNA. But an objective reason for living is not something we fashion for ourselves; nor is it something that arises from blind, indifferent forces. Objective purpose must be *given* by an intentional agent—a person. It implies an end—a goal—that has been *prescribed* for us to pursue; just as the end-purpose of a hundred-dollar bill for the exchange of goods and services, rather than for fueling fires, is what it is prescribed for it.

Meaning: Discovered or invented?

Atheists might respond that we can give our lives significance if we please—we don't need God for that. After all, they might say, whether or not a medical researcher believes in God, while seeking a cure for a deadly disease doesn't his life have meaning? Of course, anybody can experience "meaning" of a subjective kind; that is, at the level of opinion or sentiment. But the present argument is that *objective* meaning or purpose cannot exist without God—and it is this kind of purpose that humans intuitively seek.

As the atheist philosopher Thomas Nagel has recognized, "We want to matter to ourselves "from the outside." If our lives as a whole seem pointless, then a part of us is dissatisfied."[51] This is why we are more inclined to ask "What's *the* meaning of life?" rather than "What's *my* meaning of life?" We intuit that there is a reason for our existence that is meant to be discovered, not merely invented. Nagel, despite his atheist convictions, has proven to be a careful observer of the real world, which has earned him respect from theist and nontheist philosophers alike. It has also earned him severe criticism—especially from his atheist comrades. In his book *Mind and Cosmos,* Nagel explicitly rejects the usual materialist position that physics can aspire to a "theory of everything." He suggests instead that materialists *expand* their view of the physical world and consider a *teleological*—or purpose-driven—view of nature. As an alternative to brute materialism, and to better explain the subjective experience of the mind, he leans toward a view of nature that affirms "a cosmic predisposition to the formation of life, consciousness, and the value that is inseparable from them."[52] He points out that although many materialists seek a purely chemical explanation of reality, there are even staunch, card-carrying atheists like biologist Francis Crick who have admitted that events like the origin of life and consciousness seem miraculous.[53] Nagel suggests as an alternative to a miracle some form of atheistic teleology (or inherent purpose). But whereas Nagel, Crick and other materialists fight tooth and claw to avoid the God conclusion while remaining faithful to reason, believers continue to offer the explanation that fits the facts most snugly: that the observed order in nature requires the existence of a transcendent Supreme Intelligence.

The fall of Aristotle's universe

The great pagan philosophers of ancient Greece—notably Plato and Aristotle—argued that goal-directedness or *teleology* is inherent in nature. Later thinkers picked up the teleological baton and defended the idea of a "built in" purpose in nature. Medieval Christian philosophers, such as St. Albert the Great and his pupil St. Thomas Aquinas, continued the Aristotelean tradition in holding that to understand the existence of any physical thing one must ask four essential questions:

1. What is it made of?

2. What made it?

3. What makes it what it is and not something else?

4. What is it for?

These four questions corresponded to what Aristotle called the four causes of things: material, efficient, formal, and final.

Aristotle fell out of favor during the Enlightenment, when his scientific speculations were disproved by discoveries by Galileo, Newton and other scientists; but it was wrongly assumed that because his physics were faulty, so must be his *meta*physics. This led to the rejection of his notion of final causation, of purpose inherent in things, and therefore of a purpose-giver. At most, modern philosophers could accept a deistic creator who, in the beginning, "wound up" the world like a clock and let it go, blind and unguided. This God of the deists may have been a creator of sorts, but he certainly wasn't the kind to build a religion around—for, like a "deadbeat father," he was no longer around. Thus dawned an unprecedented era of religious skepticism.

In a 1948 *Atlantic Monthly* essay that has been often quoted by philosophers ever since, the philosopher Walter Stace agreed that when the Enlightenment turned its back on "final causes," the immediate consequence was the abandonment of God and religion; religious skepticism did not have to wait for the discoveries of Darwin.[54] And although belief in a purpose-driven world was prevalent throughout Christian Middle Ages, Stace asserts,

> This belief [that the world is governed by purposes] was not the invention of Christianity. It was basic to the whole of Western Civilization, whether in the ancient pagan world or in Christianity, from Socrates to the rise of science in the seventeenth century.[55]

Nonetheless, the traditional way of seeing nature—the teleological view—was increasingly abandoned as thinkers turned to a more *mechanistic* way of seeing nature. Purpose was no longer needed, they decided, to "drive" physical processes: the blind forces of nature, the particles they acted on, and the laws that governed them were all that was necessary; everything else was superfluous. According to Stace, this is not to be seen as just one of many revolutions but as "the greatest revolution in human history."[56] For it seemed once and for all to render human life meaningless, life's direction aimless, and one's existence a mere accident. Stace concludes: "If the scheme of things is purposeless and meaningless then the life of man is purposeless and meaningless too. Everything is futile, all effort is in the end worthless."[57]

A new rise in religious skepticism inevitably followed, which has persisted into the present. We can see this clearly in a contraceptive culture—our culture—where pregnancy resulting from sex is too commonly seen as an "accident," as though something has gone unnaturally wrong. But, of course, pregnancy resulting from sexual intercourse between a man and a woman indicates that something has gone wonderfully *right*, as sex is by nature procreative—and always was and always will be, no matter how

much man tampers with it. Indeed, as philosopher David Oderberg submits, "The banishment of teleology from the natural
world during the early modern period is something from which
philosophy has still not fully recovered."[58]

A Supreme Intelligence

A theory of a blind, randomly operating universe devoid of purpose might seem compelling to some. But we can verify the existence of purpose or "final causation" in nature for ourselves.
It is an intriguing fact that things seem to know what they are
doing—and predictably so. Acorns grow into oak trees, and predictably so. Electrons repel other negatively charged particles, and
predictably so. Apples do not grow feathers and fly south for the
winter, and predictably so, because it is not in their nature. The
physical universe is full of intelligible—and repeatable—cause-
effect relationships. Yet nearly all things in the universe (like
acorns, electrons, and apples) are completely unconscious. How
do they know how to be themselves and not something else? A
random jumble of materials will only end up as a house if a guiding intellect—a carpenter—intentionally causes it to happen, with
the final cause or "end" of the *completed* house in mind. One must
wonder, therefore, how it is that the inanimate objects of the
physical world—things like acorns and apples, for example, made
up of blind particles and governed by indifferent laws of nature—
behave as though they know what they are doing, as though they
have been directed by an intelligent guide. For by the very fact
that they are inanimate, they have nothing whatsoever "in mind."
St. Thomas Aquinas writes in his *Summa Theologiae*:

> We see that things which lack intelligence, such as natural bod-
> ies, act for an end, and this is evident from their acting always,
> or nearly always, in the same way, so as to obtain the best result.
> Hence it is plain that . . . designedly, do they achieve their end.
> Now whatever lacks intelligence cannot move towards an end,
> unless it be directed by some being endowed with knowledge and

intelligence; as the arrow is shot to its mark by the archer. There-fore some intelligent being exists by whom all natural things are directed to their end; and this being we call God (ST I:2:3).

Building upon Aristotle's metaphysics, Aquinas argued that such regularity and goal-directedness in the material world necessitates an intelligent "Governor," and thus the existence of God. Further, he showed that the "unmoved mover"—whom both he and Aristotle affirmed—was the same supreme intelligence behind the causal regularity in the natural world.

Unhelpfully, Aquinas's *teleological argument* for God's existence has often been wrongly equated with William Paley's *watchmaker argument,* and with modern Intelligent Design arguments. But whereas the Paley-style approaches argue for an "architect" who imposes design "from the outside," the Thomistic approach argues for a supreme intelligence that guides unconscious things toward their final causes or prescribed ends "from the inside." In other words, Paley-style arguments focus on mechanism *imposed on* nature, whereas Thomistic arguments focus on metaphysics *inherent in* nature. Paley was most concerned with nature (outside looking in), but Aquinas was most concerned with natures (inside looking out).

The Aristotelean-Thomistic approach is not at all threatened by the theory of evolution. Indeed, a person can study the secondary (or physical) causes in the universe wholly apart from the first cause of the universe. As philosopher Edward Feser writes, "The Supreme Intelligence directs things to their ends, but the system thereby created has a kind of independence insofar as it can be studied without reference to the Supreme Intelligence itself."[59] If anything, the scientific theory of evolution *complements* the Aristotelean-Thomistic approach, since evolution itself presupposes a certain goal-directedness (or final causation) in nature. Feser notes:

Even if it should turn out that animal species are the acci-dental by-products of various convergent impersonal causal processes, the existence of those evolutionary processes themselves would require explanation in terms of final causes.[60]

At the end of the day, observers must still ask: *why do these unconscious things—or unconscious processes—act as though they know what they are, what they are doing, and where they are going?* Or to put it metaphorically, why does the blind archer's arrow keep hitting the bullseye?

Our final good

If the inanimate material universe is endowed with immanent purpose, as Aristotle and Aquinas argued, then *we can reasonably expect intelligent life to be as well.* We can reject Sartre's distressing contention that human beings do not have an essence—a basic nature—that determines how we should choose to act; that "man is nothing else but that which he makes of himself."[61] We *can* affirm, to the contrary, that human life has an intrinsic nature from which built-in purpose follows. And from this we can conclude that life is meaningful, since every action we take has real meaning since it moves us toward or away from our final goal—or final *good,* as Aristotle calls it.

What is our final purpose as human persons? The answer usually given: we exist to be happy. But in what—or whom—does our final happiness lie? Where must we arrive, and what must we possess, before we can finally and forever be at rest? Christians have answered: it is the unmoved mover, the supreme intelligence, from whom all things come and in whom all things hold together; it is Jesus Christ, who in Dante's words is the "love that moves the sun and the other stars."

3

Can We Be Good Without God?

A man cheats on his fiancée the night before their wedding. A campaigning politician hires a hitman to take out his competition. A terrorist flies a plane into a skyscraper. It seems that there are at least some things that everyone considers wrong. We hear about such crimes—and we long for justice. At the deepest depths of our being we are convinced that these people *ought to* know better.

"Two things fill my mind with ever-increasing wonder and awe . . . the starry heavens above me and the moral law within me," wrote the eighteenth-century philosopher Immanuel Kant. He was impressed by both the physical reality that surrounded him and the moral reality that resided within; and much of his philosophical work was an attempt to reconcile the scientific view of reality with humanity's experience of free will and morality. Whatever else we might think of Kant's philosophy, we can all surely agree with him that we too experience moral promptings within ourselves. But not only that: we also experience a mysterious confidence that the same moral law binds *all other people* at *all times* in *all places*; that the moral law which governs us from within is an *objective* one, no less than physical laws such as gravity. Of course, there are key differences between physical laws and moral laws. Physical laws *describe* the behavior of material things; moral laws *prescribe* the behavior of intelligent beings. Physical laws describe what *is*; moral laws prescribe what *ought to* be. This distinction is helpful in explaining why science, like the physical laws it presupposes, can only ever describe what we do—but never prescribe what we *ought* to do. We can "observe" that a man *is* stealing money; but we cannot "observe" that a man *ought not* to steal money.

Our experience of "the moral law within" suggests important things about who we are as rational beings. Morality presupposes, for example, that we can think before we act; that we ought to "know better" when we do wrong. It also presupposes that, unlike the many capable but unintelligent machines that surround us, we can choose our actions freely. One would not (sanely) take his car to court after it quits and makes him late for work; nor would he sit his microwave down for an intervention after it stubbornly refuses to heat his food. Cars and microwaves are not held to moral standards—they have no *personal responsibility*—because they possess neither intellect nor free will. They are slaves to the forces of nature, as a croquet ball is to the mallet that hits it. We cannot altogether escape the forces and laws of nature ourselves, but we can, unlike machines, discover and ponder them. We can decide to live as though they exist, or we can ignore them to our own destruction. Being intelligent beings makes us responsible beings.

Finally, the existence of the moral law also tells us about who God is. It tells us that he is personal, that he is conscious and intentional, that he values certain things over others, and that he is interested in our lives. Most importantly, it tells us that he is good. But even before all that, the moral law tells us that God exists. Anyone can believe that moral truths exist—and most people do! But only the existence of God can adequately justify such belief, as you will soon see. For as Edward Feser puts it, "An atheist or naturalist can *believe* in morality—that is a psychological fact—but he *cannot* have a *rational justification* for his belief—that is a philosophical fact."[62]

No God, no goodness

No one can be good without God. But wait! Does that mean that a person needs to be religious to be good? Not at all. But though *belief* in God is not necessary for a person to act according to objective moral truths, the *existence* of God is. For if God does not exist, then neither do objective moral truths—and if that is the case then no manner of behavior can be rightly said to be objectively better than another, morally speaking. A *moral truth*—such as "it is wrong to kill other human beings for fun," or "it is good to think rationally"—is a factual statement about objective morality. So moral truths are objectively true statements about right and wrong. Collectively, they constitute what we have called the moral law.

Now let's consider a more formal version of the moral argument for God:

1. If objective moral truths exist, then God exists.

2. Objective moral truths do exist.

3. Therefore, God exists.

The formidable atheist philosopher J.L. Mackie reflected in *The Miracle of Theism* that objective, prescriptive moral facts "constitute so odd a cluster of qualities and relations that they are most unlikely to have arisen in the ordinary course of events, without an all-powerful god to create them. If, then, there are such intrinsically prescriptive objective values, they make the existence of a god more probable than it would have been without them."[63] According to Mackie, the best explanation of objectively binding moral truths is God. But since he is an atheist, he rejects such truths on account of them being too inexplicable and unintelligible in a Godless world.[64]

As the major premise of the above syllogism asserts, if objective moral truths exist then that necessitates God's existence to explain them. But the opposite is also true: if God does not exist then there is no true and objective moral law binding anyone: not atheists, not Buddhists, not Christians, not anyone. Our sense of moral values and duties in a Godless world can be grounded in nothing more than our emotions and desires. Ultimately, then, it matters not how one *feels* about actions like rape or murder; it matters not what one *thinks* about them: none of our subjective powers are powerful enough to make a moral sentiment objectively binding for one and all. So unless God exists there is no rational ground for believing in objective, mind-independent morality. Skeptics must face this hard-to-swallow fact—and many have. Agreeing with Dostoevsky, the atheist philosopher Jean Paul Sartre admits, "Indeed, everything is permissible if God does not exist, and as a result man is forlorn."[65] Or as Alex Rosenberg puts it, if atheism is true then "anything goes."[66]

What is God?

When the eminent Anglican theologian N.T. Wright was chaplain at Oxford, he would make a point of setting up a brief meeting with each of his first-year undergraduates to welcome them. The students would often say things like, "You won't be seeing much of me. I don't believe in God." Wright would then ask them which god they don't believe in. Their responses were usually telling, as they would describe a god that is nothing like the God of Christianity. Wright would then assure them, to their surprise, that he didn't believe in that god either—but in the God who is revealed in Jesus of Nazareth. "What most people mean by 'god' in late-modern Western culture," observes Wright, "simply is not the mainstream Christian meaning." The true concept of God should instill in us a desire to love God; that is, to worship him. He writes:

> The thing about painting portraits of God is that, if they do their job properly, they should become icons. That is, they should invite not just cool appraisal, but worship—though the mind must be involved as well as the heart and soul and strength in our response to this God.[67]

We should thus clarify what we mean here by "God." Classical theists understand God to be, not *a* perfect being, but perfect being itself. St. Thomas Aquinas called God *ipsum esse subsistens*, or the sheer act of "to be."[68] In other words, God has no limitations to his being, which means he has no imperfections. He is not limited by time—he is beyond or "outside of" time. He is not limited by matter or space—he is beyond them. He is beyond and therefore not limited by all physical boundaries, but present and active within them, as an author is to the story he writes. The one true God possesses every perfection to an unlimited degree. St. Thomas was able to demonstrate the fittingness of his concept of God as *pure unlimited being* through his proofs for God's existence, most notably his Five Ways.

Richard Dawkins claims in *The God Delusion* that "there is absolutely no reason to endow [God] with any of the properties normally ascribed to God: omnipotence, omniscience, goodness."[69] According to the celebrated atheist, "The five 'proofs' asserted by Thomas Aquinas in the thirteenth century don't prove anything, and are easily . . . exposed as vacuous."[70] But whereas St. Thomas devotes hundreds of pages to careful argumentation for God's existence and related questions in his *Summa Theologiae* and *Summa Contra Gentiles*, Dawkins lays out his refutation of all Five Ways in less than three pages. One cannot take Dawkins seriously on this, but for the fact that many credulous readers have. Far from an irrational assumption, God's eternality and unlimited perfection is a *logical* conclusion from arguments developed not just by Aquinas, but by the likes of Aristotle, Augustine, Plotinus, and Leibniz.[71] They and others have demonstrated what God must be like with great philosophical subtlety and rigor. Unfortunately, their arguments are often caricatured by careless critics like Dawkins. Hence, if atheists want to make *good* arguments for atheism, they must refute the right God.

What is good?

One reason no one can be objectively good in a Godless world is that without God, in whom are infinite perfections, there would be no perfect standard of goodness; there would be no way to determine what a morally good action *is*. To say that one action, person, or society is morally better than another we must appeal to a moral standard—and that standard must be *absolute*. This is where the all-good God logically makes his entrance. In daily life we refer to such absolute standards all the time. If my three-year-old daughter draws two lines on a chalkboard, we can only determine which one is "better" by referring to a perfect straight line. If we are comparing two maps of England, we can know which one is "better" only by referring to the objective standard of England itself. Likewise, we cannot say that some actions or persons or societies are morally "better" than others unless there is an objective standard of perfect moral goodness. This perfect standard of goodness—or Goodness itself—we call God.

A second reason why objective morality could not exist without God is that there would be no adequate lawgiver with the authority to impose such universally binding obligations. Anyone can make up his own moral law and impose it if he is tyrannical enough; but there is nothing objective about a moral law that has its origin in mere personal preference. What is needed is a morally perfect being who has the right to impose a single moral law that binds all men in all times and places. Without that, it would be only men themselves who would determine the moral law—or laws. But which men? Enter the dictatorship of moral relativism.

But if God is the sole moral lawgiver, doesn't that make *him* the dictator? Why should we accept *his* moral law? What makes *him* so special?

Is God a dictator?

God demands that all men obey and worship him; indeed, he created us for that purpose. What does this tell us about his character? Is his demand unreasonable? Some say so. In an online article posted by the Richard Dawkins Foundation, for example, one commentator imagines a team of behavioral experts creating God's psychological profile. The author writes:

> The following is what I think would be high on their lists. Narcissistic. God likes to be praised. If you don't praise him, he will either kill you, send you to hell or excommunicate you.[72]

Is there merit to this? Only if the God they are talking about is *not* the God of classical theism, specifically Christianity. Let's start with the charge of narcissism.

There are two root errors that lead to sin: making ourselves greater than God, and making God less than ourselves. The second error—creating God in our own sinful image—is especially at play here. To call God a narcissist is to forget that God, properly understood, has no imperfections nor limitations whatsoever. God therefore has good reason to think of himself as the only perfect being because he is, in fact, just that. To describe him as anything less is to describe a divinity inconsistent with what Christians mean by God. St. Anselm in his *Proslogion* describes God as "that than which nothing greater can be thought." Not only is God the greatest thing that exists—and thus even more than just the greatest idea ever conceived—but he is also unlimited in his greatness. He is necessarily perfect and depends on nothing outside of himself for his infinite perfection. That means that he did not need to create us; and that when he did he didn't do it for his own gain, but purely out of love

A narcissist, on the other hand, has an exaggerated sense of self-importance and therefore suffers from delusion. A person who understands himself as "the greatest conceivable being" may well be called insane. He sees the world—or wants the world to see him—in a way that does not accord with reality. But a person who understands himself to be "the greatest conceivable being" and *is* that sees what is really and truly there. He sees reality as it truly is—which is the measure of sanity. One can hardly fault God for his sanity.

Furthermore, if it were true that God was narcissistic or evil—even in light of the suffering and evil that penetrates the life of every human being—then, as Lewis suggests in *The Problem of Pain*, the fact that such a vast number of men throughout history have come to understand God as essentially *good* is mind-boggling: "If the universe is so bad, or even half so bad, how on earth did human beings ever come to attribute it to the activity of a wise and good creator?"[73] Indeed, if the God of the Bible is not good—if he is an egomaniac or a murderer or a despot—why have the majority of men believed that he *is* in fact good? If God were evil, we would expect more believers in an evil God—or more people who believe in a plurality of gods, some of whom are good and some of whom are evil. But the only ones, by and large, who seem to posit the idea of an evil god behind the universe are atheists who don't believe in *any* god. Atheists don't count as believers in an evil God or any god at all, obviously, but it is an intriguing fact that many sound as if they *do*. As Chesterton remarked, the atheist often seems to live in "an atmosphere of defiance and not of denial."[74] Perhaps this was on his mind when he wrote in the same essay, "If there were not God, there would be no atheists." Certainly this is what Lewis was thinking when he recalled some of his former atheistic thoughts in *Surprised by Joy*:

> I was at this time living, like so many Atheists or Antitheists, in a whirl of contradictions. I maintained that God did not exist. I was also very angry with God for not existing. I was equally angry with Him for creating a world.[75]

Divine revelation reveals quite a different God than the egotistical, self-serving one suggested by the fellow from the Dawkins Foundation. There is no question that the Old Covenant people understood their God to be merciful and loving. Psalm 100:4–5, for example, was recited daily by the ancient Jews as a prayer of praise and thanksgiving:

> Give thanks to him, bless his name!
> For the Lord is good;
> his steadfast love endures forever,
> and his faithfulness to all generations.

For Christians, the New Testament helps to put the goodness of God into clearer focus. As St. John the Evangelist writes: *God is love*. Not only does the Trinity exist eternally as a perfect union of divine persons, God has chosen to create other persons to share in that inner life of love. To love is to will the good of the other, which God has done by creating us, not for his good (remember that he is unlimited in perfection in himself, whether he creates or not) but for our own. Our very existence is contingent on his goodness. He seeks no advantage from having created us; rather, he wants us to share in his blessed life as sons and daughters. He wants to fulfill all our desires, but this is only possible if he as Creator is put before creation. Although God cannot increase in greatness, man can—if he can submit to the proper order of things and choose to love God first.

Consider what it means for the infinite and all-powerful God to become a finite, suffering man. By doing so, he became like us in every way except sin, suffering and dying for our sake purely out of love and according to his own will. "I lay down my life," Jesus said, "that I may take it again. No one takes it from me, but I lay it down of my own accord" (John 10:17). Narcissists do not give up their lives for the sake of others.

A narcissist, remember, has an exaggerated sense of self-importance and thus suffers from delusion. But a person who understands himself to be the greatest conceivable being and in fact *is*, sees reality as it truly is—which is the measure of sanity. The only such person is God, whom we therefore cannot fault for his sanity.

God's demand for the worship and unreserved love of every man is not arbitrary: it accords with the nature of things. Man *exists* to worship God; he lives, moves, and has his being in God, and for that reason it is right and just for him to offer his love and all he has to God, who is never outdone in generosity.

God is Good

What makes God uniquely qualified to impose a universally binding moral law on mankind? His infinite perfection. C.S. Lewis believed that our interior moral experience tells us more about God than anything we might experience outside of ourselves:

You find out more about God from the moral law than from the universe in general just as you find out more about a man by listening to his conversation than by looking at a house he has built.[76]

Furthermore, we can know from how God is—perfectly good—that he cannot will or create anything that is inherently evil.[77] Everything that God creates and commands *must* be good, if capable of corruption. In short, God creates what he loves, loves what he creates, and his commandments are always in accordance with that love. And because God in his perfection is unchanging, so are his commandments. The moral law is what it *must* be, which means that God *could* not make acts such as rape or murder morally good. His commandments are a *necessary expression* of his perfectly good, unchanging nature; he commands what is good because *he* is good. He is in fact the very locus and standard of goodness—*goodness itself.* For a Christian, then, the idea of a morally deficient God is inconceivable: his nature makes it impossible.

4

The Lawmaker Within

In a world without God all human actions can at best be reduced to matters of *personal preference* or *physical necessity*. Either we have the power to make choices but are morally ungoverned by God (according to nontheism), or we are mere bags of matter that have only the illusion of free will (according to materialism). Either way, a world that lacks a transcendent moral anchor is a world where "anything goes," and moral rules are invented rather than discovered. Even in the nontheistic view an objective moral law seems unlikely; for the god of the "spiritual but not religious" person is neither essentially good nor personal. Unless God is something very close to the God of Christianity, it is hard to make a serious case for a moral lawgiver—or at least one that we *ought* to obey. As the philosopher C. Stephen Evans argues:

> It is only the commands of a God who is essentially good who can create moral obligations. The commands of an all-powerful being who had no concern for the good would fail to create any moral obligations in humans, even if humans were created by this being.[78]

Yet our interior sense of an objective morality indicates that there *is* a "right way" to act; that there *is* a moral law that is universally binding. This inward inclination toward the "right way" is called *conscience*: that inner voice that says "do this" or "don't do that" or "you shouldn't have done that!" or "you ought to fix it." And because of it, we often find ourselves going where we do not want to go, doing what we do not want to do, or saying what we do not want to say. Yet disobeying our conscience is often more painful than obeying it. "There comes a time when one must take a position that is neither safe, nor politic, nor popular but he must take it because conscience tells him it is right," affirmed Martin Luther King Jr.[79] In other words, there comes a time when we must have moral courage and follow our conscience at any cost (and how often we hail people who do so as heroes!). Indeed, our conscience demands unconditional obedience, respect, and loyalty. Strangely, in a culture so averse to moral authorities, almost no one would say it's okay to disobey one's own conscience (can you even say "it's okay to disobey your conscience" without disobeying your conscience?). But where on earth does such authority come from? The philosopher Peter Kreeft draws the following conclusion:

> Conscience has absolute, exceptionless, binding moral authority over us, demanding unqualified obedience. But only a perfectly good, righteous divine will has this authority and a right to absolute, exceptionless obedience. Therefore *conscience is the voice of the will of God*.[80]

Cardinal John Henry Newman drew the same conclusion, calling the conscience the "aboriginal vicar of Christ."[81] He too was in awe of the mysterious authority of the conscience, and believed the best explanation for it was a supreme and personal authority, since only persons can wield authority, and only a *divine* person could have *absolute* authority over all humanity. Newman writes:

> Man has within his breast a certain commanding dictate, not a mere sentiment, not a mere opinion or impression or view of things, but a law, an authoritative voice, bidding him do certain things and avoid others. What I am insisting on here is this, that it *commands*; that it praises, blames, it threatens, it implies a future, and it witnesses of the unseen. It is more than a man's own self. The man himself has no power over it, or only with extreme difficulty; he did not make it, he cannot destroy it.[82]

But conscience is more than a feeling—what Newman, above, called "mere sentiment." Feelings (unless bridled according to right reason) are often fleeting, impulsive, and irrational. Conscience on the other hand is abiding, authoritative, and reasonable. These distinctions are key. Kreeft points out, "If our immediate feelings were the voice of God, we would have to be polytheists or else God would have to be schizophrenic."[83] Feelings may accompany our conscience, but they are not synonymous with it.

Newman suggests that a harmonious relationship between conscience and the feelings it invokes is only possible if we feel morally answerable to a person:

> If, as is the case, we feel responsibility, are ashamed, are frightened, at transgressing the voice of the conscience, this implies that there is One to whom we are responsible, before whom we are ashamed, whose claim upon us we fear . . . These feelings in us are such as require for their exciting cause an intelligent being: we are not affectionate before a stone, nor do we feel shame before a horse or a dog.[84]

Through our conscience we discern not only an abstract moral law but a personal moral lawgiver. When we transgress our conscience, we feel we have let someone down. On the other hand, when we obey our conscience—particularly if it requires great courage—we feel as though we have been praised. Our brains, which are mere things rather than persons, neither praise nor blame. The feelings we experience when we respond to our conscience derive from our relationship with a personal being who is holding us accountable.

It follows then from our experience of conscience that it is not necessary to know where the moral law *comes from* to know the difference between right and wrong. A child can know what light is long before he learns about electromagnetism. So religion is not necessary *in practice* to leading a morally upright life. But that is not to say that religion has no valuable part to play in the formation of one's moral understanding. If you are feeling adventurous and decide to camp out in the Amazon rainforest for a week, you can do so left to your own inadequate devices—or you can accept instruction and accompaniment from a guide whose resources go far beyond your own. Clearly, you'd be wiser to take the latter route.

I would be remiss if I were not to make a further point: conscience—operating as a sort of "voice of God" in our soul—can never be contrary to reason; nor can it ever be contrary to what the Catholic Church teaches. In his famous Regensberg Address, Pope Benedict XVI emphasized that God's action is *always* reasonable. His divine nature necessitates it. Or put another way, God can never act contrary to reason. Thus, "Christian worship is worship in harmony with the eternal Word and with our reason." And we can further apply this principle to our topic of conscience: *Christian action is action in harmony with the eternal Word and with our reason.*

Our conscience, therefore, must be *formed* according to what is true. A poverty-stricken mother who believes her conscience is telling her to abort her expectant child "for the child's own sake" has a malformed conscience. She is not really hearing God's voice, but a perversion of it. What this means, then, is that to properly hear and follow our conscience we must ask ourselves what is the most reasonable course of action. But secondly, in view of our fallible intellects, we must always be prepared to subordinate our imperfect minds to the infallible teaching authority of the Church Christ founded—the Catholic Church, which is the official interpreter of the Word of God, and the "pillar and bulwark of truth" (1 Tim. 3:15). The Church, then, serves to form our consciences more perfectly and completely than we could on our own. At this point one may wonder whether such a Church exists. But he should at least admit that if such an infallible authority were to exist, then it would surely make sense for every person interested in living "the reasonable life" to become its pupil.

Where does the moral law come from?

Most skeptics will readily acknowledge the objective evil wrongness of crimes such as child abuse or rape. What many probably don't realize is the implications of such an admission—because if objective rights and wrongs exist, then so must God. But even in lesser matters of right and wrong, the skeptic unwittingly affirms objective morality—like when the local banker butts in front of Mr. Skeptic in the hot-dog line at the fair, or when little David loads up his new sling shot to use Mr. Skeptic's windows for target practice. Surely Mr. Skeptic will demand that David *ought* to have known better, that it is wrong to damage personal property for fun. And if he didn't know this moral truth, his parents *ought* to have taught it to him. It is not just that Mr. Skeptic *dislikes* the selfish behavior of the banker, or having his windows broken. His personal dislikes aside, he *disapproves* of these things because they break the moral law.

Where does such a standard or law come from? Why should others be held to Mr. Skeptic's moral standards? What makes Mr. Skeptic's moral law so special?

Those who want to avoid a supernatural lawgiver but want to affirm the existence of objective moral truths are forced to attribute them to either man or nature. Some take the position that man collectively, as a society, determines the moral law. Whatever the majority believes at a given time and place—that is what constitutes the moral law *for that society*. But a "majority wins" method for determining objective morality cannot be infallible. Who wins, for example, if a society is split fifty-fifty on a particular moral question? Then who decides? If the Nazis had conquered the entire world and brainwashed every person on earth to accept their anti-Semitic worldview, would worldwide acceptance of anti-Semitism be justified? Of course not. Majority opinion does not decide the moral law. No merely socially determined standard of morality provides a basis for one society to criticize another's—for that is *their* moral law, not ours, and who are we to impose *ours* on *them*? Without a single moral standard for *all* societies, universal moral progress would be impossible and moral laws would be reduced to mere social conventions, akin to laws about which side of the road to drive on. C.S. Lewis sums it up:

"If the Rule of Decent Behavior meant simply 'whatever each

nation happens to approve,' there would be no sense in saying that any one nation had ever been more correct in its approval than any other; no sense in saying that the world could grow morally better or morally worse."[85]

How about nature as the source of objective morality? Can human moral experience be explained in purely evolutionary terms? This is the default position for many skeptics. In their view, morality is useful in keeping us from killing each other before the next generation of offspring can be produced. It seems more than plausible that an "anything goes" society completely ungoverned by a common moral code would be hostile to human survival and reproduction. So, if the moral law is sociologically and biologically advantageous, perhaps it is nature which imposes such a moral law.

But a moral law which has biological and societal advantages is perfectly *compatible* with theism. To begin with, the theory of evolution does not exclude the possibility that a God exists who is concerned with human morality. Indeed, God could be the guiding hand behind natural selection. "Mr. Darwin's theory need not then to be atheistical, be it true or not," wrote Cardinal Newman. "It may simply be suggesting a larger idea of Divine Prescience and Skill."[86] In the same spirit, Pope Benedict XVI affirms the compatibility of the religious view of the world with the theory of evolution:

We cannot say: creation or evolution, inasmuch as these two things respond to two different realities. The story of the dust of the earth and the breath of God, which we just heard, does not in fact explain how human persons come to be but rather what they are. It explains their inmost origin and casts light on the project that they are. And, vice versa, the theory of evolution seeks to understand and describe biological developments. But in so doing it cannot explain where the "project" of human persons comes from, nor their inner origin, nor their particular nature. To that extent we are faced here with two complementary—rather than mutually exclusive—realities.[87]

Since evolution is fully compatible with religions like Christianity, we might then ask whether it would be in God's power to give moral commandments which happen to be socially and biologically advantageous *as well*. For as Newman suggested, such a compatibility between creation and evolution would magnify rather than stifle God's omniscience and omnipotence. As the philosopher Mitch Stokes reflects:

> I have no doubt that our moral code(s) provide survival advantage over many of the alternatives. But this biological benefit does not in itself imply that our ethics developed naturalistically. It may be, for example, that a divine Lawgiver hardwired us with knowledge of moral laws, and one of the benefits of following them is that things will generally go better for us, as well as for others.[88]

So the naturally advantageous results of following our conscience may be the result of God's careful planning. It might be tempting to reach for Ockham's razor at this point. Perhaps this just sounds like we're superfluously adding God into the picture. But that is not the case at all. An evolved moral code is not the same as an objective moral code. Evolution could only explain why certain actions are naturally *advantageous*; not why certain actions are objectively right or wrong. Remember the major premise of the moral argument: if God does not exist, then objective moral truths do not exist. And as Stokes affirms, "According to the evolutionary story, our moral beliefs are merely survival tools, not the apprehending of eternal truths."[89] So at best, if evolution is the only explanation for our moral convictions, then what appears to be an objective moral law written on our hearts is really only evolved moral sentiments. And if objective morality is reduced to mere sentiment rather than law, then who is to say we ought not to go against them if we "feel like it"? Consider these remarks by ethicist Peter Singer and biologist Marc Hauser:

It is important for us to be aware of the universal set of moral intuitions so that we can reflect on them and, if we choose, act contrary to them. We can do this without blasphemy, because it is our own nature, not God, that is the source of our species morality.[90]

It all comes down to whether *objectively* some things are really right and wrong, or whether or not *objectively* "anything goes." For Hauser and Singer, because they don't recognize a God who has instituted a moral law, anything goes.

It follows from nature's incapacity for prescribing an objective moral law, that if objective moral truths do exist, *they must have a supernatural source.* For even if scientific advancement reached perfection and every physical fact about the universe became known to man, we would still not have a moral law. Even if our scientific knowledge became so complete that we knew the whole universe inside and out, we would still know nothing about what *ought* to be—we would only know what *is.* You can observe that a man is being tyrannical; but you can never observe that a man ought not to be tyrannical. Let us say, then, that the moral laws are not objects in the physical world. The moral law is transcendent; it is beyond us. Yet it weighs down upon us, and urges us from deep within. It is a mysterious thing, yet utterly real and immanent in our experience. The moral law must, therefore, be grounded in something supernatural, because nature is silent about right and wrong.

Morality and religion

The first question we must ask about God, once we have established that he exists, is whether he is worthy of worship. The reasonableness of religion stands or falls on this question.

As C.S. Lewis recognized, we can tell a lot about God from our experience of the moral law. Moral truths impose value on our actions, for instance; but value (like purpose) can only be imposed by a conscious, intentional value-giver. In his book *The Moral Landscape*, atheist neuroscientist Sam Harris concedes this point when he writes, "Let us begin with the fact of consciousness: I think we can know, through reason alone, that consciousness is the only intelligible domain of value."[91] In other words, *real* value always requires a mind to do the valuing. Gold only becomes a "precious" metal once a value has been conferred upon it. Gold has no intrinsic value, and it cannot give itself value. Without an intelligent value-giver, therefore, gold is worth no more than coal. Whether we are talking about inanimate objects or human actions—or human beings, for that matter—nothing can have more value than another unless a conscious value-giver has made it so. Thus, we can expect God to be a conscious person who takes a special interest in how we live our lives from moment to moment.

So not only does an objective moral law only make sense if an objective standard of goodness exists—but that standard or locus of morality must also be *personal*. Law makes no sense without a lawgiver. Even some atheist philosophers are willing to admit this, but it creates a quandary for them. The atheist Richard Taylor, for instance, wants to affirm objective morality. But who are the rule-makers, he asks? He observes that *"permitting, forbidding,* and *requiring* are themselves expressions of activities, or things that people do. We are therefore led to ask: who is it that thus permits, forbids, or requires that certain things be done or not done?"[92] Indeed, as Taylor recognizes, a *binding* moral code only makes sense if a *person* has placed value—positive or negative—on the given actions. "If a given action is described as wrong and therefore forbidden," he proposes, "it seems the most obvious next questions should be, Forbidden by whom?"

But Taylor still needs to make sense of our deep-seated intuition that all are bound by a common moral standard. Since he cannot attribute objective morality to an almighty God, or to an "almighty" human person, all he is left with is nature. He must defer to the explanation that makes the least sense. Thus Taylor (and any other nontheist who wants to affirm objective morality) is forced to conclude that "since there appear to be no lawmakers superior to those that are human, then . . . we must suppose that

moral right and wrong are just part of the fabric of nature itself, however inherently implausible this bizarre supposition may
seem."[93] But as we have seen, the source of the moral law—the
moral lawgiver—*must* be personal. Nature does not fit that bill.

The divine attributes uncovered in natural theology—that
God is good and personal, for instance—can illuminate for us
the reasonableness of Judaeo-Christian worship. N.T. Wright's
definition of worship is simple and true: "worship means, literally, acknowledging the worth of something or someone." Well,
God is of infinite worth, for he is both infinitely good and *our*
ultimate good. It is truly right and just, always and everywhere,
to worship *this* God—and this God alone.

In a culture where "freedom" means being able to do whatever you want rather than what is right, the idea of religious
submission has become repugnant. To today's New Atheists, a
God who demands worship appears as nothing less than tyrannical and narcissistic. To others, worship just seems inconvenient, boring, a lesser form of opium. Modern man's intense
resistance or indifference to worship is surely based—at least in
many cases—on a misunderstanding of the *real* God and his *real*
nature; not to mention on a misunderstanding of himself. Sanity
begins with the realization that God does not need us to worship him—*we* need to worship God. Worship cultivates peace in
the soul of the deepest and most lasting kind. *When we worship,
we rest.* It is thus the essential human activity, the first of all first
things, and the secret to real and lasting happiness.

Man exists to worship God and is obligated to do so, precisely
because man is man and God is God. We cannot avoid it: we
will all worship something. That is, we will all accept *something*
as our highest good. Why not accept the Highest Good as your
highest good? Because if there are good reasons to believe that
such a being exists, this is the only reasonable option. *For man
becomes like whomever he worships*; and in that simple statement is
the secret to why religion matters.

PART II

Why Worship Jesus?

Even on the cross he did not hide himself from sight; rather, he made all creation witness to the presence of its Maker.

—St. Athanasius, *On The Incarnation*

5

The Search for a Visible God

Believing in invisible things can be difficult. When things are shielded from our senses it is easy to be indifferent to them. This is why many tobacco companies have been required to show images of the visible effects of smoking (such as a blackened lung) on their packaging; it is easier to break a dangerous habit when its harmful effects are made visible to us.

I remember when my wife, Amanda, and I found out we were expecting our first child. Over the next few weeks we would often look at her belly and remark, "I can't believe we have a little baby in there!" We walked by faith and not by sight before the first prenatal ultrasound. As the weeks went by Amanda started to feel sick and tired, and eventually she could feel the baby's little kicks. It wasn't long before I could too. Then we had our first ultrasound and *saw* our baby for the first time. After that, things became more real for me—and yet not as much as you might expect.

At first I had difficulty accepting that our new baby existed. There was plenty of evidence that it did, but I was not especially excited about it. It was as if the baby's existence was hypothetical. I felt guilty for not *feeling* more excited.

But things became very real to me in the third trimester. When little Anna was finally born and became present to all my senses, I found myself utterly in love. The invisible had burst into plain view. This experience helped me to appreciate how hard it can be to believe in what is unseen. This is especially true about believing in God, who all too often seems *too* hidden for a God who is supposed to be active at all times in our lives. Even the Psalmist lamented God's apparent hiddenness: "How long, O Lord? Wilt thou forget me forever? How long wilt thou hide thy face from me?" (Ps. 13:1).

Where is God?

Although believing in something invisible can be difficult, worshipping it is far more so. People today tend to be most interested in things that are present to their senses. God is not one of them. His hiddenness is, for many, a barrier to faith, and understandably so.

Yet many of us remain, even today, profoundly spiritual if not religious. Perhaps this is because God is not as hidden as he seems. Maybe we somehow sense his presence, if only "in a general and confused way," as St. Thomas put it (ST I:2:1). Every human person seeks the fulfillment of all his desires, yet he can't find it in this life. But to quote Thomas again, "a natural desire cannot be in vain" (ST I:75:6). The total fulfillment of all our desires must be possible; and since it doesn't happen in this life, it must be waiting for us in the next. This was, in a nutshell, C.S. Lewis's argument from desire. But the point for now is this: maybe God has indeed made himself known, however indirectly, to every person in order to draw them to him at their own pace and on his own time.

Now it cannot be denied that God is not accessible to our physical senses. But the same goes for historical facts, moral truths, and metaphysical truths that we nevertheless accept as real. And as we saw in Part I, although God remains inaccessible to us physically, he makes his presence and activity in our lives apparent through our intellectual capacities: through *reason* and *experience*.

Now let me say a little bit about the relationship between reason and mystery. Our intelligence is unlike God's because God knows *all* truths and holds nothing false to be true. But we can still come to know many truths. In other words, we can think *like* God—just not *as* God. Could it be, then, that we are sometimes too hasty in faulting God for not acting as we expected him to—as *we* would have acted if *we* were God? To think with omniscience and act with unlimited power is beyond our capability (imagine an ant trying to understand particle physics). We cannot fill God's shoes. Nor can his "brain" fill our heads. We want to make complete sense of God's actions, yet we too easily forget that his thoughts are not our thoughts, nor his ways our ways (Is. 55:8–9). Faith is accepting reason as far as it goes, while accepting whatever reason points to beyond itself. Chesterton famously remarked, "The poet only asks to get his head into the heavens. It is the logician who seeks to get the heavens into his head. And it is his head that splits."[94] The truth is, all of us have a little bit of the logician and the poet inside us. For Chesterton, the poet is not unreasonable; he is just not exclusively logical. He leaves room for mystical truth that cannot be reasoned to. Indeed, Chesterton goes so far as to say that the poet is the *most* reasonable of men because of what poetry is: a means of "expressing the inexpressible." The poet not only thinks to his rational limits; he goes *beyond* what his reason has told him. A truly reasonable person, then, is open to both rational proofs and mysteries. Even Aquinas, arguably the greatest Christian thinker who ever lived, remarked after a profound mystical experience that all he had written in his lifetime "seemed as straw" compared to the mysteries of heaven—and he never wrote another word. Chesterton was right: the riddles of God are more satisfying than the solutions of man.[95]

All this to say that it is entirely reasonable to admit the limits of our reason when it comes to God's hiddenness; and it is just as reasonable not to resent the fact. Of course, we are never justified in surrendering our reason outright; for that would be subhuman. We are right, on the other hand, to surrender the expectation that we can know everything about everything. We reason as far as we can, building momentum, then we coast into mystery.

Not that one should merely and automatically punt to "mystery" when it comes to the problem of divine hiddenness. We are within our rights to speculate about what good reasons God might have for remaining beyond our sense experience. The God of Christianity desires man to seek him (and to find him). We know this because he said it: "Ask, and it will be given you; seek, and you will find; knock, and it will be opened to you" (Matt. 7:7–8). This is not a promise that God will grant everything at our immediate request, like a genie; only the *right* thing on *his* time according to *his* will.

The problem of reasonable atheists

Proponents of the divine-hiddenness argument betray an interior desire to believe in God, and a commitment to do so on one condition—that he provide the right evidence. Which brings up another crucial point: is there such thing as perfectly open-minded atheists, or nonbelievers who genuinely desire to believe in God? And if there are, why doesn't he make it easy for them? Couldn't he just show himself and be done with it? This variation on the problem of divine hiddenness might be called *the problem of reasonable nonbelievers*. Used as an argument against God's existence, it has been robustly defended by atheist philosopher J.L. Schellenberg. He argues that if God exists, he must be perfectly loving. But a perfectly loving God would make his existence unmistakably evident to anyone who is open to it. Since there are nonbelievers who are open to God's existence but, through no fault of their own, have failed to find grounds to believe in him, we must conclude that he does not exist. This argument is a fair one and has persuasive force, but, as with atheist arguments from the problem of evil, the theist can provide plausible answers.

Can we be sure that there are any nonbelievers who are as inculpable in their doubt as Schellenberg assumes? Are there really nonbelievers who are willing to consider the evidence and arguments for God, and to follow them wherever they lead? It's not as if solid philosophical arguments for God's existence are hard to find. From Aquinas's Five Ways to Alvin Plantinga's "Two Dozen (Or So) Theistic Arguments" to the "Twenty Arguments for God's Existence" compiled by Peter Kreeft and Fr. Ronald Tacelli, there is an abundance of strong arguments for God's existence and against atheism. Many of them have proven their persuasive power by making believers out of committed nonbelievers (notable examples include C.S. Lewis, Francis Collins, and Antony Flew). Moreover, men throughout history have come to belief in God without ever hearing a philosophical argument; they have been able to intuit God's existence from the truth, goodness, and beauty they have experienced in the world around them.[96] Skeptics may be quick to dismiss this, but reasoning to belief in God from personal experience is no less rational than coming to belief through argument. Indeed, the rationality of belief based on experience has been robustly defended by first-rate philosophers such as Alvin Plantinga and William Alston. The point here is that convincing reasons for belief have never been hard to find. Thus, one might wonder where reasonable atheists are looking, and whether their failure to look in the right place is really through no fault of their own.

There are, no doubt, open-minded atheists who are prepared to be converted to belief by knock-down arguments. But for Pascal, mere preparedness or openness to God's existence was not enough. One must actively "look" for God with the mind and heart if he wants to decisively encounter him. Pascal argued that God desires only those who really seek him to see him. In his *Pensées* he wrote, "He has willed to make himself . . . appear openly to those who seek him with all their heart, and to be hidden from those who flee from him with all their heart. He so regulates the knowledge of himself that he has given signs of himself, visible to those who seek him, and not to those who seek him not."[97]

But even if there were reasonable nonbelievers, God would still have reasons to *postpone* direct revelation of his existence to a non-believer. The analytic philosopher Peter Van Inwagen proposes that we not lose sight of the fact that *why* we believe may be more important to God than *that* we believe.[98] If God were to provide signs and wonders to, say, 100 atheists at once, this might prove his existence to all 100, but it might not lead to 100 new personal relationships. Some might still choose to turn their back on God; they might "believe and shudder."[99] Timing is crucial. Because one can believe in God without desiring a personal relationship with him, he might withhold immediate evidence of his presence until a more fitting time in a person's life—or he may reveal himself subtly and gradually. He may allow us to experience suffering and doubt—and not just experience these things but choose freely between good and evil, and whether to seek God or not—so that we may *develop* into creatures who are more morally excellent, and more able to follow his will when he does make his existence clearer to us. This is what the philosopher John Hick calls the "soul-making process";[100] and this, perhaps, is why God does not immediately create us as perfect heavenly creatures with no "earthly phase of existence," suggests philosopher Michael Murray.[101] A man who has struggled for his own success—one who has *persevered* and shown good character—is always more honorable than he who has had everything handed to him on a silver platter.

So to quote Pascal again, "God wishes to move the will rather than the mind."[102] Perhaps God has given us just enough evidence to keep us *interested* in him, that we might continually seek him and be forged in faith, like steel through fire, along the winding way of life. Moreover, by remaining discoverable but not obvious, he provides us an opportunity to help one another arrive at belief. Even as the evangelists, this provides an opportunity to come to greater faith through our own struggle and choice, as we encounter the difficult questions and doubts of the one we are evangelizing. Again, maybe God remains just hidden enough to compel us along a path mixed with doubt and discovery, but that ultimately leads to our higher perfection. Why shouldn't God give us some role and personal accountability in such a project? Good fathers don't do *everything* for their children; sometimes they act only as guides until their intervention is needed.

A hidden reality

Sometimes we fail to notice things because they are *too close* rather than too far (like our noses!). Proximity can increase obscurity. "A prophet is not without honor," said Jesus, "except in his own country, and among his own kin, and in his own house" (Mark 6:4). It was often the people closest to Jesus that had the hardest time seeing who he really was. St. Augustine famously mused in his *Confessions* that God is closer to us than we are to ourselves. This is only possible because of his utter transcendence: he dwells in all things, not physically, but metaphysically (*beyond* the physical). God is *ipsum esse subsistens*; he is "being itself"; therefore, all existing things (you, me, the trees outside your window, etc.)

are grounded in the sustaining action of God. Thus, no thing or person is—or ever could be—more intimate to us than God. The Thomistic philosopher Etienne Gilson expressed this essential truth in what he called "The Great Syllogism":

1. Being is innermost in each thing.

2. But God is being.

3. Therefore God is innermost in each thing.[103]

C.S. Lewis offered a solution—if not to quell then at least to soften—the problem of hiddenness by arguing that in a limited way God reveals himself to every person through our awareness of the moral law, and the force of conscience. The Canadian philosopher Travis Dumsday defends Lewis's argument and draws out its implications as follows:

> For Lewis, we encounter transcendence first and foremost in the transcendent moral law, accessed via conscience. . . . In a sense then, while God is not immediately and in all his fullness directly accessible via the conscience (such that this second strategy of reply does not strictly contradict the first) . . . our awareness of the moral law does provide us immediate epistemic contact with eternal transcendent reality: the law itself. That law in turn points to the Mind in which the law resides.[104]

If such a thing as a moral law exists (and we have seen that there are good reasons to believe it does), then we have evidence that a transcendent, personal lawgiver exists and is present to us in a mysterious but tangible way. Lewis, like Cardinal Newman, believed that our conscience was best explained by a transcendent, authoritative person—or "issuer of instructions," as Dumsday puts it. Affirming this line of reasoning, he writes:

> The moral law itself transcends the natural order; moreover, through the law we have a clear indicator that there is yet

something else behind the physical world, something much more like a mind than like anything physical, as only something mind-like could be the ultimate repository and issuer of instructions.[105]

There are no good reasons to doubt that deep moral intuitions are a universal human experience. Every conscious, thinking person experiences the weight of conscience, the sense of a moral law written on their heart that compels them to act—and judge—accordingly. Thus we might argue that God has revealed himself directly to *every* person through interior moral experience. The experience of conscience is not likely enough to overwhelm a person to full-blown Christian belief; but it is at least a catalyst for faith in a present, personal God who wants us to be reasonable and good, and who, we would be warranted to conclude, must possess such qualities himself.

But for some, such non-sensual evidence is not good enough. They insist that God be literally palpable and visible; they want an *incarnation* of God. Yet there are good reasons to believe that God has, in fact, already given us just that in the person of Jesus of Nazareth who (ancient biographers tell us) was born of a virgin, possessed wisdom that awed even the educated, turned water into wine, multiplied loaves and fishes, read minds, prophesied and fulfilled prophecies, calmed storms, performed exorcisms, restored the dead to life, triggered radical conversions, performed countless physical healings, and loved like only God could love. Yet people *still* disbelieved in him, going so far as to torture and crucify him. Yes, God *did* show himself to us, two thousand years ago—but we killed him.

Perhaps, one might argue, Jesus should have made his divine identity more obvious and undeniable. Instead, he spoke in parables. He answered questions with questions. He urged witnesses to keep his miracles secret. He frustrated his interrogators with willful silence. But perhaps all the signs necessary for belief were there all along. It is as though Jesus desired his identity to be hidden *just enough* to baffle those who were not willing to see and accept the signs.

But regardless of why Jesus did things the way he did, every person must face the startling possibility that maybe God *has* after all shown himself to the world in a way fully palpable; perhaps God *has* revealed himself in Jesus Christ, the roving miracle-worker and founder of the world's largest and most resilient religion. Indeed, billions of Christians through the centuries have believed that this is so. They have come to believe in Christ as true God and true man, and as the reason for hope in a world marred by sin and suffering. They have discovered that, despite his hiddenness here and now, Jesus is the definitive solution to the problem of evil and suffering. For it was Christ who, two thousand years ago on a hill near Jerusalem, turned the worst crime ever committed into a saving sacrifice: the once-for-all sacrifice that conquered sin and redeemed the world. Therefore, the best thing we can do is entrust our lives to the mercy of God. The worst thing we can do is go on as if nothing happened.

The problem of evil

The crucifixion of Christ is a profound reminder of the reality of evil in the world. We may thus, at this point, briefly draw to mind what many agree is the most formidable of impediments for believing in God: the problem of evil. How could an all-knowing, all-powerful, all-loving God allow evil and suffering in the world he created? Different variations of this problem have been formally proposed as an argument against God's existence since long before Christ. Clearly, it is also closely related to the problem of divine hiddenness. Together, the problems of evil and divine hiddenness constitute the most *emotionally* powerful arguments against the existence of God. But despite this, they can be reconciled theologically, logically, and experientially.

One modern convert from atheism who has wrestled with the problem of evil and suffering is Francis Collins. As the former director of the Human Genome Project and the current director of the National Institutes of Health, the largest supporter of biomedical research in the world, Dr. Collins is unquestionably a reasonable man. Both his interest in science and his religious skepticism were fully awakened during his graduate studies. He recalls: "I went off to be a graduate student in quantum mechanics at Yale, where I was very compelled with the notion that everything in the universe can be described in a [mathematical] equation. . . . I concluded that, well, if there was a God, it was probably somebody who was off somewhere else in the universe; certainly not a God that would care about me. And I frankly couldn't see why I needed to have any God at all."[106] Religious indifference had taken its hold.

Eventually Collins went into medicine. Still a skeptic, he was nonetheless deeply impressed by how his suffering patients who—even while facing terrible diseases and the poorest of prognoses—received great consolation from their religious beliefs. They were *convinced* that there was meaning and purpose beyond what this life has to offer, and their heroic witness began to undermine Collins's skepticism. "I had made a decision to reject any faith view of the world without ever really knowing what it was that I had rejected," admits Collins. "And that worried me. . . . As a scientist, you're not supposed to make decisions without the data. It was pretty clear I hadn't done any data collecting here about what these faiths stood for." So he went looking for "the data" and found the writings of C.S. Lewis, in particular Lewis's moral argument for God's existence, which was "[the] most surprising, most earth-shattering, and most life-changing. . . . How is it that we, and all other members of our species, unique in the animal kingdom, know what's right and what's wrong? In every culture one looks at, that knowledge is there. . . . I reject the idea that that is an evolutionary consequence".[107] Both the witness of faith and hope provided by Collins's patients, and his discovery of the moral argument for God, played key roles in overcoming his atheism.

Both these discoveries are critical for coming to terms with the problem of evil. Let's look at the moral argument first. Its major premise, as already discussed, asserts that if objective moral truths exist then God exists. But we could also put this in the negative: if God does not exist, then there is no adequate basis for objective morality; and if there is no such basis, then it follows that there are no grounds for declaring anything really and objectively evil. So either both God and evil exist, or neither exist. *There cannot be a problem of evil unless evil really exists.* Therefore, the problem of evil is more of a problem—a difficulty, but not a defeater—for the believer in God than for the unbeliever. On the other hand, the real problem for the atheist is that there is *no* evil in the real world—at least if atheism is true.

The *logical* problem of evil has been proposed since centuries before Christ, perhaps most famously in the ancient world by Epicurus in the third century B.C. The idea is that the existence of a good, all-powerful God and the reality of suffering are as logically inconsistent as a married bachelor. It is logically *impossible*, therefore, that both God and suffering exist. Philosophers and theologians have thought about this problem for millennia, but despite the emotional appeal of the argument, no one has been able to decisively prove that God could not preside over a world like ours where people suffer—especially if by accepting and persevering in our sufferings in this life, we are promised an unimaginably greater good in the next. Infinite happiness in the next life is infinitely greater than finite suffering in this life. The atheist philosopher William Rowe thus concedes, "Some philosophers have contended that the existence of evil is logically inconsistent with the existence of the theistic God. No one, I think, has succeeded in establishing such an extravagant claim."[108] Other prominent atheists such as J.L. Mackie and Paul Draper have made similar admissions.

A better argument, I think, is the *evidential* problem of evil, which holds not that God's existence is impossible given the suffering in the world (especially innocent or unnecessary suffering), but that God's existence is *improbable*. But still, once we get past the emotional appeal of this argument it is far from airtight. For one thing, (as has already been mentioned) the atheist does not have grounds to believe in objective evil in the world; actions or events that appear evil can really be no more than unpleasant or undesirable, since no God exists to ground objective morality.

Second, we are not in a good position to know how probable it is that a good God and evil co-exist.[109] We experience reality in successive moments of time, and with limited, fallible intellects—whereas God, who is all-knowing and all-powerful, sees and orchestrates all events in one singular "moment" from eternity. How can we be so sure that God does not have good reasons for allowing human beings to freely commit evils, or even permit what appears to be pointless suffering in the world?

Third, the God of the Bible does not promise comfort and worldly success in this life. The point of this life is to grow in love for God and neighbor—and love often *requires* suffering—so that we can enjoy perfect happiness with God and neighbor for all eternity. So if Christianity is true, then the probability of the coexistence of God and suffering in this life should increase!

Finally, there are a number of solid arguments for theism—ontological, cosmological, teleological, moral arguments, and even the historical case for Christ's resurrection—that as standalone arguments provide powerful evidence for God's existence, while as a package deal of probabilities provide *all the more* a sweeping evidential argument for the existence of God. None of this is to say that evil is neither real nor even scandalous to believers and nonbelievers alike. We have all likely felt, at one time or another, that God has forsaken us. But although the logical and evidential arguments from evil should provide considerable pause to theists, they can rest assured that they do not succeed philosophically in defeating the powerful case for the existence of a good God who is worthy of obedience and worship.

The impact upon Francis Collins from his encounter with patients who held on to a supernatural faith and hope may hint at the most effective solution to the problem of evil: the experiential or *existential* solution. It is remarkable that despite the universal presence of evil and suffering in every civilization throughout history—especially when Christianity was just getting off the ground—billions of people have still chosen to believe in a loving God. What could explain this? Perhaps it is the interior experience of believers—the internal witness of the Holy Spirit—that explains how religious people can suffer yet *not* abandon God. Furthermore, understanding the nature of God—that he is the pure act of being itself—helps us to grasp how it is that God can console us and instigate within us the supernatural hope that strengthens us in the face of great suffering. The Lord does not now suffer alongside us (although Christ once did); his divine nature allows him power to do more than that. Indeed, as our creator and sustainer he is able to do something much more intimate and loving. Priest and theologian Herbert McCabe puts it beautifully:

> We can say in the psalm 'The Lord is compassion' but a sign that this is metaphorical language is that we can also say that the Lord has no need of compassion; he has something more wonderful, he has his creative act in which he is 'closer to the sufferer than she is to herself.'[110]

With this in mind, then, we can also say that God knows our suffering more than we know it ourselves.

The Christian trademark of suffering heroically has always been a potent catalyst for conversions to the Faith. That is why, as Tertullian wrote, "the blood of the martyrs is the seed of the Church." And that is why Christianity has always been a scandal and folly to the world: because in our weakness we are made strong (2 Cor. 12:9). In death and through Christ, we become victorious over evil and suffering. So you might say that the definitive solution to the problem of evil lies, not so much in an abstract argument, but in the existential *experience* of the one true and merciful God.

6

The Jesus Conspiracy

Catholicism asserts with force and conviction that God really and truly became man and kicked up dust as he walked the sands and soils of ancient Palestine. About this belief we call the Incarnation, the distinguished historian Christopher Dawson writes, "The history of the human race hinges on this unique divine event which gives meaning to the whole historical process."[111] If this doctrine is true, then Dawson is right: the Incarnation must be considered the central event in all of history. Thinking about history without reference to the Incarnation is like thinking about World War II without reference to Hitler.

Of course, there are many who deny the Incarnation. Some deny not only that Jesus was truly God, but even that he existed. Such people, called *mythicists*, often argue that certain parallels between the Gospel accounts of Jesus' life and the stories of figures in ancient mystery religions suggest that the early Christians invented Jesus, stealing details from these ancient myths. Some have called this the "copycat" argument. Unfortunately, more and more people in recent years have accepted this argument at face value, without conducting any research of their own to confirm its validity. As a result, they walk in blind faith, themselves holding to a myth that is steeped in fake history and bad philosophy.

Zeitgeist

A few years ago I received a Facebook message from my brother. It contained a link to a video called *Zeitgeist: The Movie* and the question, "What do you think of this?" I was intrigued, especially because this particular brother of mine was usually uninterested in talking religion. I clicked on the link, the film began, and I heard a voice intone:

The more you begin to investigate what we think we understand, where we came from, what we think we're doing, the more you begin to see we've been lied to. We've been lied to by every institution. What makes you think that the religious institution is the only one that's never been touched?

A few seconds later a quote from an amateur nineteenth-century Egyptologist and poet, Gerald Massey, flashed on the screen:

They must find it difficult . . .
Those who have taken authority as the truth,
Rather than truth as the authority.

Then the film launched into its assault on the historicity of Christ. Its chief claim was that the Christian religion is an *invented* religion, derived from ancient cults. It argued that many key details of the Gospels—the Virgin Birth, the twelve apostles, the death and resurrection of Christ, and so on—were not unique to the New Testament but in fact borrowed from other mythology and other religions. And if all this was invented, then the odds are that Jesus was invented too. I was shaken. Could it be true? Is Jesus, after all, a mere fiction? Have over two billion Christians (just in our own time) been duped?

At the time of my brother's message, I was still in a spiritual no-man's-land, struggling to figure out what I believed and what I did not. I had not yet learned how to sift carefully through historical claims like these. Initially, this case against the historicity of Christ caused me no little anxiety. Over time, however, I came to learn that these mythicist claims were more than dubious—and that indeed, they were no longer taken seriously by even the most skeptical scholars of ancient history. Let's look at some reasons why.

For starters, the mythicist theory is based on what is called the *false cause* fallacy, also known as the *post hoc ergo propter hoc* fallacy, meaning "after this, therefore because of this." Here's a formal representation:

Premise: X occurred before Y

Conclusion: Therefore, X caused Y

An example of this would be: "My wife ate a bowl of oat-meal, then fainted. Therefore, the oatmeal caused my wife to faint." This could be true (it could have been some kind of extreme allergic reaction); but more evidence must be provided to validate it. And this is exactly the case when it comes to the mythicist charge against Christianity. That pagan mystery cults existed *before* Christianity does not prove it to be a copycat religion—no matter the similarities. More evidence is needed; mere parallels are not enough. Consider the 1898 novel *Futility* by Morgan Robertson, which tells of a ship—the largest of its day—called the *Titan*. Although said to be unsinkable, it hits an iceberg in mid-April and sinks. Unfortunately, it carries only the bare minimum number of lifeboats, so most of its passengers perish. The parallels to the *Titanic*—even in their names—are astonishing, right? Yet we would never think to say that the real-life story of the *Titanic* was somehow based on the novel's *Titan*. Likewise, parallels between pagan mythology and Christianity cannot prove that one *caused* the other.

Moreover, many of the supposed parallels between pagan mythology and the Gospels are not as impressive as advertised. Sir James Frazer, in his well-known book *The Golden Bough*, argued that there were explicit parallels between Jesus' death and resurrection and "dying and rising gods" such as Adonis, Attis, and Osiris. Many of today's skeptics accept that theory. But as Paul Rhodes Eddy and Gregory Boyd point out in their magisterial study *The Jesus Legend*, the "rejection of the existence of a 'dying and rising gods' pattern among ancient Mediterranean religions has become a virtual consensus over the last half century."[112] Why? Because, as Eddy and Boyd point out, "in the case of each proposed 'dying and rising god,' further study revealed that either there was no death, no resurrection, and/or no 'god' to begin with." They use the Greek mythological figure, Adonis, as an example of this loose and deceptive use of language:

> In the case of the two different mythic traditions of Adon-is—once heralded as the paradigm example of a "dying and rising god"—in one myth there is no death, and in neither is there a resurrection. Rather, Adonis undergoes bilocation, spending part of the year in the upper world and part in the lower world.[113]

No one has been more thorough in contrasting the Christian sense of "resurrection" with the pagan sense of "rising" than the British theologian N.T. Wright in his book *The Resurrection of the Son of God*. When considering the supposed parallels between Jesus' resurrection and the "rising" of the gods of the mystery cults, he writes:

> Did any worshipper in these cults . . . think that actual human beings, having died, actually came back to life? Of course not. These multifarious and sophisticated cults enacted the god's death and resurrection as a metaphor, whose concrete referent was the cycle of seed-time and harvest, of human reproduction and fertility.[114]

Wright's bottom line is this: the Judaeo-Christian view of resurrection was entirely different from any other concept of "rising" in the pagan cults. Not only was the Christian conception different in substance, but to the Greco-Roman world such an event was an impossibility—even an absurdity. Resurrection in the Christian sense indicated neither resuscitation nor a mere redefinition of death—and it did not mean simply life after death; it meant a complete reversal of death, that is to say, life *after* life after death:

> The great majority of the ancients believed in life after death . . . but other than within Judaism and Christianity, they did not believe in resurrection. "Resurrection" denoted a

new embodied life which would follow whatever "life after death" there might be.[115]

It is contrary to all evidence to think that Christ's resurrection was plagiarized from a pagan religion. That hypothesis has been soundly debunked. There is no historical indication that the ancient Jews stole *anything* from myths or other religions; indeed, they resisted pagan religious ideas, wanting to set themselves apart from other religions (that's what the Mosaic Law was all about). The earliest Christians—who were largely converted Jews—shared this aversion to paganism. As Bible critic and atheist Bart Ehrman writes, "Anyone who thinks that Jesus was modeled on such deities needs to cite some evidence—any evidence at all—that Jews in Palestine at the alleged time of Jesus' life were influenced by anyone who held such views."[116] In fact, as the biblical scholar Bruce Metzger has pointed out, it is more likely that pagan religions were influenced by Christianity, trying to "stem the tide" of its rapid growth. Metzger writes: "One of the surest ways would be to imitate the teaching of the Church by offering benefits comparable with those held out by Christianity."[117] Indeed, most of our evidence for the Greco-Roman mystery religions comes from the second to the fourth century A.D.—*after* Christianity was founded. As the German historian of religion Martin Hengel has observed, "The great wave of the oriental mystery religions only begins in the time of the empire, above all in the second century." [118] The notion of Christianity being a first-century invention based on pagan mystery religions is further undermined by the fact that the earliest critics of Christianity, such as the anti-Christian philosopher Celsus and the satirist Lucian, never challenged the historical existence of Christ, basing their attacks on the assumption that he did exist, becoming "hostile witnesses" to the gospel.[119]

Fortunately, the evidence for Jesus' historical existence is more than sufficient to convince nearly every New Testament expert in the world today, including the most skeptical. Among those notable critics is Ehrman, who contends unabashedly despite his atheism: "The view that Jesus existed is held by virtually every expert on the planet."[120]

A conspiracy of silence?

When it comes to Jesus' existence, N.T. Wright affirms, "It is quite difficult to know where to start, because actually the evidence for Jesus is so massive that, as a historian, I want to say we have got almost as much good evidence for Jesus as for anyone in the ancient world."[121] But there are some who say the exact opposite. Some skeptics, such as the mythicist Earl Doherty, argue that if Jesus was truly who the Gospels say he was, we should have more evidence of his existence from the ancient historical record. "The Gospel Jesus and his story are . . . missing from the non-Christian record of the time. Philo of Alexandria, the Jewish historian Justus of Tiberius, Pliny the Elder as collector of reputed natural phenomena, early Roman satirists and philosophers; all are silent."[122] Doherty calls this "a conspiracy of silence."

Now this is a contention worthy of serious attention, but there is an even more important question. When putting together the pieces of the historical puzzle of Jesus' life, what matters above all is not *how much* evidence we find, but *how good* the evidence is. Quality over quantity. Even Doherty's phrase "a conspiracy of silence" is misleading, because although we would love to have testimony from Philo, Justus, and the like, we have plenty of credible testimony from *other* early, non-Christian sources. Indeed, as Wright says, "we have got almost as much good evidence for Jesus as for anyone in the ancient world." This means that if critics like Doherty want to doubt Jesus' existence based on what is lacking in the historical record, they would need (in order to be consistent) to doubt the existence of basically every other figure of antiquity.

So, what do the non-Christians say about Jesus? This is an important question because non-Christians have nothing to gain from affirming Jesus or the Christian faith. Historians generally consider neutral or adversarial testimony to be more valuable

than "friendly" testimony. So early non-Christian testimony—
and the earlier, the better—is essential to building a case for the
historical Jesus. Early non-Christian sources that testify to the
life of Christ, either directly or indirectly, include the writings
of Thallus, Mara bar Serapion, Pliny the Younger, Suetonius,
Celsus, Lucian of Samosata, Tacitus, and Josephus. Thallus, for
instance, refers to unusual darkness that came over the earth
when Jesus was crucified; Mara bar Serapion and Lucian refer to
Christ's execution; and Pliny confirms the persecution of early
Christians and that they worshipped Jesus as a god. All these
sources have historical value, but foremost among them are Josephus and Tacitus.

Flavius Josephus was a Jewish historian of singular importance. His *Antiquities of the Jews,* written in the first century
A.D., contains two passages that mention Jesus. One passage
refers to "the brother of Jesus, who was called Christ, whose
name was James," which, if authentic, confirms the existence of
both Jesus and his brother James (who, as per Catholic teaching,
was not a blood brother but a cousin or stepbrother of Jesus).[123]
Although some scholars assert that this short passage was added
by a Christian interpolator, there are good reasons to doubt that.
One is that Jesus and James are mentioned merely in passing,
rather nonchalantly; one would expect a Christian interpolator
to make more out of them. Another argument for the passage's
authenticity is that in A.D. 248 Origen refers to this passage in
the *Antiquities*—available at the time in public Roman librar-
ies—in his public refutation of Celsus.[124] He would not have
done so unless he believed pagan readers would accept the passage as an original part of Josephus's work.

Josephus's more important passage in the *Antiquities*—called
the *Testimonium Flavianum*—has been the subject of remarkable
attention among scholars, and for obvious reasons:

> About this time there lived Jesus, a wise man, *if indeed one ought
> to call him a man.* For he was one who performed surprising deeds
> and was a teacher of such people as accept the truth gladly. He

won over many Jews and many of the Greeks. *He was the Christ.* And when, upon the accusation of the principal men among us, Pilate had condemned him to a cross, those who had first come to love him did not cease. *He appeared to them spending a third day restored to life, for the prophets of God had foretold these things and a thousand other marvels about him.* And the tribe of the Christians, so called after him, has still to this day not disappeared.[125]

In this passage it is hard to deny the presence of some Christian "injections" embedded in the text. Scholars generally agree on the inauthenticity of three elements of the passage (italicized above): the insinuation of Jesus' divinity, the reference to Jesus as Messiah, and the reference to his resurrection on the third day. But there are strong reasons to believe that the rest of the passage is still authentic. Certain turns of phrase would not be expected of a Christian interpolator—calling Jesus a "wise man," referring to his miracles as "surprising deeds" (which suggests magic rather than divine power), and referring to Christians as a "tribe." With all that in mind, Eddy and Boyd conclude:

> While the manuscript tradition of the *Testimonium* of Josephus clearly has been tampered with, a solid case can be made that the original passage depicted Jesus as "a wise man" who performed wonders, was crucified under Pilate, and whose followers inexplicably continued to follow him after his death.[126]

Finally, we turn to the Roman politician and historian, Cornelius Tacitus. He is the author of the *Annals* and the *Histories,* both of which survive today, though only in part. The portion that most concerns historical Jesus scholars comes from the *Annals,* and was likely written around A.D. 115:

> Consequently, to get rid of the report, Nero fastened the guilt and inflicted the most exquisite tortures on a class hated for their abominations, called Christians by the populace. Christus, from whom the name had its origin, suffered the extreme

penalty during the reign of Tiberius at the hands of one of
our procurators, Pontius Pilatus, and a most mischievous superstition, thus checked for the moment, again broke out not
only in Judaea, the first source of the evil, but even in Rome,
where all things hideous and shameful from every part of the
world find their center and become popular.[127]

One reason this passage is significant is that it confirms a
couple of key historical details in the Gospels; specifically, it
confirms that Jesus was crucified during the reign of Tiberius,
and by the authority of Pontius Pilate. Again, some critics hold
the passage to be a Christian interpolation, but there is no serious evidence for this. On the contrary, it is quite unlikely that a
Christian would refer to Christianity as "a most mischievous superstition," and one that fosters "hideous and shameful" actions.
Furthermore, it is unlikely that a Christian interpolator would
write of the Crucifixion without mentioning the Resurrection.

Naturally, Christians interested in the historical case for
Jesus wish there were more references to Jesus in non-Christian
writings, but there are at least three good reasons why this is
not so.[128] First, much of the literature from the ancient world
has been lost; it is entirely possible that more was written about
Christ than we are now aware of. Second, it was not nearly as
easy to make a name for oneself (intentionally or not) in the
ancient world as it is today: information was spread primarily
by word of mouth. Third, as the biblical scholar and priest John
Meier has written, "Jesus was a marginal Jew leading a marginal
movement in a marginal province of a vast Roman Empire."[129]
Although we *now* know that Jesus' mission was one of a kind, at
the time of Christ there were a myriad of religious figures and
movements throughout the Empire. Even if pagan historians
had heard of Jesus, there is a good chance they would not have
taken much notice of him.

All things considered, then, there is more than adequate evidence for the historicity of Jesus.

7

Jesus and the Gospels

"You take too many things for granted! You can't start with God. *I don't accept God!*" These were the words of twenty-one-year-old C.S. Lewis to his friend, Leo Baker, shortly after the Second World War. Both Lewis and Baker had been commissioned officers and wounded in action, and were equally convinced of their opposite positions on God's existence. Baker recalls[130] another time when he asked his feisty atheist comrade whether he was afraid while fighting in France, to which Lewis replied, "All the time, but I never sank so low as to pray."

At the height of his atheism Lewis found himself a lowly victim of something akin to the "unyielding despair" once described by Bertrand Russell. "Nearly all I loved I believed to be imaginary," wrote Lewis, "[and] nearly all that I believed to be real, I thought grim and meaningless."[131] Clearly, at that point it might have seemed to Lewis's peers that a conversion to Christianity was next to impossible. But Lewis not only became a Christian; he also became one of the most influential Christian apologists of the twentieth century. In *Surprised by Joy,* Lewis recalls how, as he began to take religion more seriously, he deliberated over which religion might be *the* true one. It came down to Hinduism and Christianity. Eventually he accepted Christianity over the former. The decisive consideration was the overpowering personality of Jesus Christ.

Every religion in some way brags of its affiliation with some highly significant personage, whether it be a founder, prophet, or sage. Buddhists have Buddha, Muslims have Muhammad, Hindus have Gandhi, Jews have Abraham. What makes the Jesus of Christianity tower above these? First, he was a worker of miracles:[132] he multiplied bread and fish, calmed storms, read minds, read hearts, walked on water, cured illnesses, resuscitated the dead—and rose from the dead three days after being brutally tortured and executed. Second, he claimed to be on equal footing with the creator of the universe; he was the only founder of a world religion who claimed to be God. At least that's what the Gospels tell us. But can we trust the Gospels?

A quadrilemma

Religious skeptics, critics, and indifferentists toward Christianity rarely cast Jesus in a bad light; to the contrary, they usually credit him with being a wise man or moralist. This was even the case during the strongly antireligious Enlightenment. In his seminal study *At the Origins of Modern Atheism*, the Jesuit theologian Michael Buckley notes:

> In the Enlightenment the distinction [was made] between Christianity and Christ. . . . No one denied the moral genius of Christ. . . . The Enlightenment agreed that Jesus was a Jewish ethical preacher, still illuminating a world in which tradition and Church had distorted his beliefs and maxims beyond recognition.[133]

This peculiar tendency to *reduce* rather than reject Jesus persists today. No person, however, can call Jesus a mere wise man or moral teacher and stop at that, no matter how great they say he was. The Gospels are clear: *Jesus claimed to be God*; and if Jesus was not *that* then he was anything but a man of "moral genius"; he was a liar and a cheat—or just insane. Lewis develops this argument famously in his classic, *Mere Christianity*:

> I am trying here to prevent anyone saying the really foolish thing that people often say about Him: I'm ready to accept Jesus as a great moral teacher, but I don't accept his claim to be God. That is the one thing we must not say. A man who was merely a man and said the sort of things Jesus said would not be a great moral teacher. He would either be a lunatic—on

the level with the man who says he is a poached egg—or else he would be the Devil of Hell. You must make your choice. Either this man was, and is, the Son of God, or else a madman or something worse. You can shut him up for a fool, you can spit at him and kill him as a demon or you can fall at his feet and call him Lord and God, but let us not come with any patronizing nonsense about his being a great human teacher. He has not left that open to us. He did not intend to.[134]

Captured here is Lewis's famous "Lord, Liar or Lunatic?" trilemma. Many have found this approach interesting, even persuasive. It certainly is a neat and simple way to nudge any honest inquirer into serious thought about who Jesus was—and is. But there is a fourth question: whether Jesus is just a *legend*. We have already explored this question with respect to whether he even existed. But even if it is conceded that he did, we still face the question: was he anything like what the New Testament portrays him to be?

The Gospels are historical biography

If we can establish that the Gospel writers—Matthew, Mark, Luke, and John—were intending to write history and not, say, mythology or some other literary genre that is less likely to record "the facts" about Jesus' life, then we have reasonable grounds to believe that the Gospels are an accurate portrayal of the Jesus of history.

The first time I encountered the historiographical evidence for the Jesus of the Gospels, I was still in university, a somewhat confused and uncommitted skeptic. My roommate and best friend regularly attended a men's Bible study and would, on occasion, encourage me to tag along. I always had an excuse to decline, until one day when he caught me in a moment of weakness (perhaps Holy Spirit–induced) and I agreed to attend. So off we went. It was an uncomfortable experience. As a sort of cultural Catholic at best, my Bible at this time served as little more than a bed-table ornament, and its contents were all but meaningless to me. Since my experience of male community was mostly in the locker room (I was a university football player), the religious enthusiasm and sensitivity with which these guys spoke during their discussion was off-putting. There was no swearing, no chauvinistic talk—I was not used to this. Annoyed and in a hurry to leave after it was over, I was putting on my shoes when the leader of the study came over, shook my hand, and smiled, "So glad you could make it, Matt!" I retorted reflexively, "Are there even any good reasons to believe that Jesus was a real person? I mean, is there even one book or resource out there that could make that case?" I was nearly certain the answer was no. "Wait one minute," he said, and ran upstairs. He returned quickly with a copy of Lee Strobel's *The Case for Christ*. (Strobel is an award-winning law journalist—and former atheist—who, as a professed skeptic, famously interviewed several of the world's most prestigious New Testament scholars. His goal had been to disprove Christianity once and for all, especially to his wife who was, at the time, a new convert. Strobel succeeded, not in debunking Christianity, but in dissolving his own atheism.) "Take this and see what you think," the Bible study leader said confidently, handing me the book. Reading it was the first time I saw how truly compelling the historical case for Christ was, and that belief in Jesus didn't have to be based on feelings alone.

There are good reasons to trust the Gospels. To see this, we should start by asking the simplest of questions: What are the Gospels? Are they history, like Josephus's *Antiquities* and Tacitus's *Annals*? Are they biography, like Plutarch's *Lives*? Are they fictional stories? This last question has been explored most comprehensively by the biblical scholar Richard Burridge. Largely because of his work, many recent scholars have conceded that the Gospels are most in alignment with the genre of *Greco-Roman biography*.

Catholic biblical scholar Brant Pitre summarizes five key features that the New Testament Gospels share with ancient biography.[135] First, ancient biographies focus on the life and death of an individual, focusing primarily on the individual's public career and very little on birth and childhood. Second, they average between 10,000 and 20,000 words in length; all four Gospels fall in this range. Third, they often begin with ancestry or genealogy. Fourth, ancient biographies are often not in chronological order, but are organized topically or thematically. Finally, ancient biographical works are not exhaustive: they do not intend to provide *every* detail about what their subject did or said; and as to the latter, they do not intend to convey to a verbatim transcript, only the *substance* of what the person said.[136] With considerations such as these in mind, scholars such as Graham Stanton have concluded, "I do not think it is now possible to deny that the Gospels are a subset of the broad literary genre of 'lives,' that is, biographies."[137]

We also have good reason to conclude that the Gospel writers intended to write historical biography. This is evident by the fact that they *say so*. The clearest example is the prologue of St. Luke's Gospel, which begins:

> Inasmuch as many have undertaken to compile a narrative of the things which have been accomplished among us, just as they were delivered to us by those who from the beginning were eyewitnesses and ministers of the word, it seemed good to me also, having followed all things closely for some time past, to write an orderly account for you, most excellent Theophilus, that you may know the truth concerning the things of which you have been informed (1:1–4).

Scholars have acknowledged the striking similarities between Luke's prologue and those prologues of other important ancient historians. Also, Luke states his commitment to historical truth clearly: he intends to compile a narrative of things that have been accomplished; he has obtained information from eyewitnesses; he has followed all things closely; and he desires to write an orderly account so that the reader may know the truth. Luke could not have been more direct about what he was up to. His integrity as a historian has been tested time and time again, both with respect to his Gospel and his Acts of the Apostles, and the conclusions have been consistent: Luke displays the qualities of a first-rate historian of the ancient world.

We can safely conclude that the Gospel writers intended to accurately portray the life and sayings of the historical Jesus, while packing those same writings with theological richness. Thus, they are what Pope Benedict XVI calls "interpreted history."[138] Indeed, "The old ideas that the Gospels are not biographies but folklore and fairy stories completely fail to reckon with the literary evidence."[139]

The historical reliability of the Gospels

We have established so far that there are good reasons to believe Jesus existed and that the Gospels of the New Testament best fit the genre of historical biography, meaning that they are intended to accurately convey true history. The next question is, do they succeed in that? Are they in fact reliable?

The New Testament scholar and historian Michael Licona has identified five common objections to the historical reliability of the Gospels (what he calls the "ABCDE" approach):

Authorship

Bias

Contradictions

Dating

Eyewitnesses

Let's begin with the *authorship* objection. Some scholars say we should be wary of trusting the Gospels because the original manuscripts (called "autographs") were anonymous. They had no titles or headings, and no authorship attribution. The Gospels were not associated with Matthew, Mark, Luke, and John—contend these critics—until long after the originals were published, as much as a century.

But this argument lacks credibility. As both Licona and Pitre have pointed out, the earliest manuscripts we have are not anonymous. In fact, there is no good reason to think that any anonymous manuscripts have *ever* been found. Period. Furthermore, the attribution of the Gospels in the early Church was unanimous: Matthew was always attributed to Matthew, Mark always to Mark, and so on.

What kind of manuscript evidence do we have for the New Testament? More than enough to make a Christian want to jump up and down, clapping his hands with childlike delight. Over 5,000 Greek manuscripts exist, containing all or part of the New Testament. In addition, we have over 10,000 manuscripts in other languages like Latin and Syriac. The earliest copy is probably the John Rylands papyrus—a fragment of the Gospel of John—which many scholars date to the first half (some to the first quarter) of the second century. The earliest complete manuscript of the Bible, the *Codex Vaticanus*, is dated to around the middle of the fourth century. In addition, virtually the entire New Testament can be reconstructed just from quotations by the early Church fathers.

Finally, note that three of the Gospel authors would be unlikely choices if one wanted to construct a false Gospel. Only John is a credible candidate for that, since he is the only one of the three who is shown to be especially favored by Christ, as one of the Lord's "inner three" along with Peter and James. Matthew was favored by Christ in that he was called as an apostle, but he was also a former tax collector (not a trusted or esteemed occupation in first century Palestine). Mark and Luke were not apostles at all. Pitre writes:

> If authority is what you were after, why not attribute your anonymous Gospel directly to Peter, the chief of the apostles? Or to Andrew, his brother? For that matter, why not go straight to the top and attribute your Gospel to Jesus himself?[140]

The bias objection

Next, let's look at the *bias* objection. Skeptics will sometimes contend that the Gospels are propaganda, clearly meant to lead the reader to religious conversion. They point to passages like the one at the end of St. John's Gospel, which openly states that the miracles of Christ "are written *that you may believe* that Jesus is the Christ, the Son of God" (John 20:31). To be sure, the potential for bias is not to be ignored when evaluating evidence. But does bias automatically rule out the reliability of a document? No.

In the preface to *The God Delusion*, Richard Dawkins states openly, "If this book works as I intend, religious readers who open it will be atheists when they put it down." By stating such an aim, Dawkins has not undermined his arguments: he has merely given the reader a clearer understanding of his intentions, but the arguments must speak for themselves. Indeed, everyone who desires to make an argument for something *must* have some bias in favor of what they are setting out to prove. Clearly, bias alone is not enough to discredit the Gospels.

Contradictions in the manuscripts?

Third, we have the *contradictions* objection. Scholars have counted up to 400,000 variants in the extant manuscripts of the New Testament. On its face, this number is striking—even alarming. But experts also have concluded that over ninety-nine percent of these variants are insignificant to the meaning of the text. Most variants are as inconsequential as one manuscript saying "Jesus Christ" and another saying "Christ Jesus." Moreover, the more manuscripts and fragments we have (and for the New Testament we have thousands) the more variants we should expect. As apologist Trent Horn points out, there is only one manuscript copy of the first six books of Tacitus's *Annals*. Although historians treat this manuscript as very important when it comes to gaining information about ancient Rome, Horn also notes, "It has no variants, but that's only because there are no other copies for the text to differ with! This is a very bad thing, because we have no way to know if this manuscript represents what Tacitus originally wrote."[141] Therefore, it is actually quite remarkable that despite their variants there is so much uniformity among the New Testament manuscripts.

What about the small percentage of variants that are considered more significant? Here is what scholar Craig Blomberg has concluded:

> Only about a tenth of one percent are interesting enough to make their way into footnotes in most English translations. It cannot be emphasized strongly enough that *no orthodox doctrine or ethical practice of Christianity depends solely on any disputed wording.*[142]

Blomberg mentions skeptical scholar Bart Ehrman's admission that "essential Christian beliefs are not affected by textual variants in the manuscript tradition of the New Testament."[143] It seems, then, that the argument against New Testament reliability on the grounds that there are contradictions among the various manuscripts does not carry much weight. At the end of the day, any of us who encounter Bible or manuscript difficulties would do well to heed the advice of St. Augustine:

> The authority of these books has come down to us from the apostles through the successions of bishops and the extension of the Church, and, from a position of lofty supremacy, claims the submission of every faithful and pious mind. If we are perplexed by an apparent contradiction in Scripture, it is not allowable to say the author of this book is mistaken; but either the manuscript is faulty, or the translation is wrong, or you have not understood.[144]

Dating

Our fourth consideration is the *dating* objection. Skeptics will sometimes contend that the Gospels were written too long after the events they record. There was ample time, therefore, for the information to get blurred or distorted. One of the big issues here is the mistrust many modern critics have with oral tradition. It is true that the Gospels are dated by most scholars from the 60s to the end of the first century. Mark's Gospel is often (but not always) assumed to be the first; the Gospel of John is almost always believed to be the last. But all of the Gospels were written within the lifetime of the apostles, meaning they could have—and would have—been corrected by disciples of Christ if inaccurate.

But what about *before* the first Christian writings, when the Gospel was passed on by oral preaching? Can the oral tradition of the earliest Christians be trusted? Some skeptics use the "telephone game" analogy to justify their skepticism. The telephone game goes like this: a sentence or phrase gets whispered from one person to another around a circle until it finally reaches the last person, who says it out loud and everyone has a good laugh at how distorted it has become—for instance, "My nose is dripping. I have a bad cold" becomes "My new sis is tripping. I hate bat coal." But is this sort of distortion what would have happened with the oral tradition of the early Christians? Not likely.

Distortion of the original Gospel texts is unlikely, first, because as Craig Blomberg points out, "Eyewitnesses of Jesus' ministry, including hostile ones, could easily have refuted and discredited the Christian claims if they were in any way mistaken."[145] Blomberg also points to the work of German scholar Rainer Reisner, an expert on the educational methods common to ancient Israel and neighboring areas. Reisner lays out several good reasons to assume that the early Christians would have preserved Jesus' works and sayings accurately, even if not memorizing them word for word. First, he argues, Jesus spoke as the prophets did in the Old Testament, proclaiming the word of God with authority, so his followers would have wanted to preserve his teachings carefully. Second, Jesus presented himself as the Messiah, though often obscurely. At least some of his disciples—such as Peter, who confessed to Jesus, "You are the Christ, the Son of the Living God!"—recognized to some degree who he really was. Third, Jesus used easy-to-remember forms of communication: he often spoke in parables, and used vivid imagery and figures of speech. Fourth, Jesus commanded the apostles to transmit his teachings to others. Fifth, education for Jewish boys until at least age twelve was common in the first century, and often involved rigorous memorization of the Torah and other books of the Old Testament. Lastly, observes Reisner, it was the norm for teachers in the Jewish and Greco-Roman world of the first century to gather disciples around them for the specific purpose of perpetuating their teachings. It is reasonable to believe that Jesus, no matter how unique a teacher he was, would have had the same intention.

There are, therefore, good reasons to believe that not only were the Gospels written early enough to be considered reliable by the standards of historians of antiquity, but that oral tradition would have accurately transmitted Christian teachings before they were written down.

Eyewitness testimony

Lastly, there is the *eyewitness* objection—that is, that the Gospels lack reliable eyewitness testimony. But there are good reasons to discredit this objection. John claims explicitly to be an eyewitness, writing at the end of his Gospel:

> *This is the disciple who is bearing witness to these things, and who has written these things*; and we know that his testimony is true (John: 21–24).

His status as a true eyewitness is validated immediately afterward by Christians who wanted to affirm "that his testimony is true." Biblical scholars Scott Hahn and Curtis Mitch write, "Apparently this comment was inserted, not by the evangelist, but by other Christians who knew the facts about Jesus as John did and willingly testified to the veracity of his Gospel."[146]

In his prologue, Luke explicitly states that he has been in contact with "those who from the beginning were eyewitnesses"; he has at the very least *interviewed* eyewitnesses. Although secondhand, then, Luke's Gospel can still be considered eyewitness testimony. He writes:

Inasmuch as many have undertaken to compile a narrative of the things which have been accomplished among us, just as they were delivered to us by those who from the beginning were eyewitnesses and ministers of the word" (Luke 1:1–2).

Comments New Testament scholar Richard Bauckham, a significant player in defending the credibility of the Gospels as eyewitness testimony: "Luke can tell the story 'from the beginning' because he is familiar with the traditions of those who were eyewitnesses 'from the beginning.'"[147] The idea that Luke has spoken with those who were with Jesus "from the beginning" is very significant. For instance, he seems to know intimate details about the angel Gabriel's appearance to Mary, including her inner response—as when he writes that, upon being greeted with "Hail, full of grace," she "considered in her mind what sort of greeting this might be" (Luke 1:29). It seems likely, therefore, that Luke at some point sat *face to face* with Mary, the mother of Jesus, and heard her direct narrative of the things that had occurred.

Lastly, one might wonder if the Gospel writers, whether as eyewitnesses themselves or as interviewers of eyewitnesses, would have forgotten or mixed up some of the details. Bauckham explains why this is unlikely:

> The eyewitnesses who remembered the events of the history of Jesus were remembering inherently very memorable events, unusual events that would have impressed themselves on the memory, events of key significance for those who remembered them, landmark or life-changing events for them in many cases, and their memories would have been reinforced and stabilized by frequent rehearsal, beginning soon after the event.[148]

That Jesus was a worker of extraordinary deeds is certainly emphasized by the Gospels. In fact, miracles concerning Jesus—especially the Virgin Birth and Resurrection—are a focal point of the entire New Testament. This is one reason why some skeptics consider the Gospels historically unreliable; they distrust them because of their miraculous content.

But it was not unheard of for ancient historians (including Herodotus, the "father of history") to include miraculous or legendary events in their histories. Still, these works are considered valuable by modern historians because much in them is still considered reliable historiography. Moreover, non-Christian sources also confirmed Jesus' reputation as a miracle worker of sorts. Many ancient writers granted that Jesus worked wonders but made differing attempts to explain such deeds. The Jews attributed his works to sorcery or demonic powers. Celsus, a ferocious opponent of Christianity, contended in his *True Doctrine* that Jesus was a sorcerer and a magician.[149] Significantly, *no* early sources flat-out deny that Jesus worked wonders.[150]

But Jesus was more than a miracle worker—he claimed equality with God, identifying himself as "I am," the name of God revealed to Moses (Mark 6:50; John 8:58; Exod. 3:14). He also claims to be "lord of the Sabbath" (Matt. 12:8; Mark 2:28). Furthermore, Jesus *acts* as though he is God. Jesus confirms his self-understanding as one equal with the Almighty by forgiving sins on his own authority—something first-century Jews knew only God could do.

He also teaches the Torah with an authority transcending that of even the greatest rabbis, using phrases like, "You have heard it said . . . but I say . . ." (Matt. 5:17–48). That is why at the end of Mark's Gospel the high priest rends his garments and accuses Jesus of blasphemy (Mark 14:53–65). It was not blasphemy to claim to be the Messiah; but it *was* blasphemy to claim equality with God, which is exactly what Jesus does, time and time again, in word and in action, throughout the Gospels. And that is why the deeply respected Jewish scholar and rabbi Jacob Neusner concludes after reflecting on the Jesus of the Gospels: "I now realize, only God can demand of me what Jesus is asking."[151]

8

Death and Resurrection

Imagine three historians—a Christian, a Jew, and an atheist—are locked in a university library and are only allowed to re-emerge once they have formed a consensus on the indisputable historical facts about Jesus' life, what some historians call *historical bedrock*. Such an agreement would be incredibly valuable, since the Jew and the atheist are non-Christians and, therefore, have no Christian axe to grind. Such "enemy" testimony is generally held to count more than biased testimony when attempting to confirm historical claims.

Recognizing the importance of "enemy testimony," New Testament historian Gary Habermas has sought to determine (1) which historical facts about Jesus are well-evidenced, and (2) which facts are agreed upon by most New Testament experts, Christian and non-Christian. Habermas has called these points of agreement "minimal facts."[152]

The first minimal fact we will look at is Christ's crucifixion. "That [Jesus] was crucified is as sure as anything historical can ever be," affirms the generally skeptical New Testament scholar John Dominic Crossan.[153] Islamic scholars reject the crucifixion of Christ because the Quran (Surah 4:157–158) teaches that Jesus *was not* crucified. But this is, of course, heavily biased, and not supported by the strongest available evidence—as we'll see. Nor is it even close to the majority view. Outside of Islamic scholarship, acceptance of the crucifixion of Jesus as historical bedrock is nearly unanimous. And there is no evidence from ancient sources denying the crucifixion. Then, as now, it was widely accepted as a historical fact.

Why do historians find evidence for the crucifixion so convincing? To begin with, the Gospels are important historical sources *whether or not* they are accepted as inspired Scripture.

All four Gospels attest to the crucifixion and death of Christ.[154] Luke is clear in his prologue that he is setting out "to write an orderly account for you . . . that you may know the truth concerning the things of which you have been informed" (Luke 1:1–4). Furthermore, the Gospels portray a Jesus weakened even to the point of crying out, "My God, my God, why have you forsaken me?" (Matthew 27:46). G.K. Chesterton recognized the sheer *scandal* of these words, uttered by a bloodied and broken-bodied Messiah, when he wrote: "Let the atheists themselves choose a god. They will find only one divinity who ever uttered their isolation; only one religion in which God seemed for an instant to be an atheist."[155] In interesting contrast, Jewish martyrs in other ancient accounts were usually depicted as strong and brave in the face of torture and death. "In light of these," concludes historian Michael Licona, "reports of a weaker Jesus at his arrest and crucifixion could cause embarrassment in contrast."[156] The Gospel writers, after all, want their readers to believe that Jesus is God; showing him to be weak would seem to work against that. Scholars therefore consider the Crucifixion unlikely to have been fabricated.

Other New Testament books and letters (some of which are dated earlier than the Gospels) also refer to Jesus' death, some specifying crucifixion as the mode of execution. Non-canonical Christian sources also confirmed the crucifixion of Jesus. Worthy of special mention, however, is St. Paul's first letter to the Corinthians, written around A.D. 55. In this epistle he acknowledges the crucifixion event explicitly, and does so in the form of an oral tradition, or *creed,* that had already been circulating among Christians (1 Cor. 15:3–7). This creed, according to at least one major New Testament scholar,[157] originated as early as *months* after Christ's death. Though some scholars would not be quite so generous, most of them, secular and Christian, agree that this creed can be dated to within five years of Jesus' crucifixion.

Non-Christian sources also attest to the crucifixion of Christ. As seen earlier, the first-century Jewish historian Josephus writes about "[w]hen Pilate, upon hearing [Jesus] accused by men of the highest standing amongst us, had condemned him to be crucified."[158] The Roman historian Tacitus records in his second-century *Annals* (15.44) that "Nero fastened the guilt and inflicted the most exquisite tortures on a class hated for their abominations, called Christians by the populace. Christus, from whom the name had its origin, suffered the extreme penalty during the reign of Tiberius at the hands of one of our procurators, Pontius Pilatus."[159] There are also other early non-Christian sources that allude either directly or indirectly to Christ's crucifixion, including writings by Lucian of Samosata, Mara Bar Serapion, and (as a secondary source) the Babylonian Talmud. Usually, historians concerned with substantiating events in the ancient world drool over even *two* early, independent sources. It suffices to say, then, that the historical evidence for the crucifixion is well established—enough to convince even the most skeptical historians.

The scandal of the Passion

But why crucifixion? Couldn't God have saved us some other way? Consider the emotional lamentation of Richard Dawkins in a 2012 debate with Australia's Cardinal George Pell: "It's a horrible idea that God, this paragon of wisdom and knowledge and power, couldn't think of a better way to forgive us our sins than to come down to Earth in his alter ego as his son and have himself hideously tortured and executed so that he could forgive himself." But no one is claiming that God *had* to atone for our sins in precisely this way; of course, the all-powerful God could have atoned for the sins of man in a less traumatic, less bloody way.

Jesus could have atoned for our sins any way he wanted; indeed, he atoned for our sins in exactly the way he wanted. God does nothing in vain. He did not *need* to suffer and die on the cross; he chose to. And by doing so, he taught us in the profoundest way the gravity of sin, man's desperate need of salvation and, above all, the infinite depths of his love for us.

Did Jesus really die on the cross?

Now, anyone who knows anything about Jesus will know that his story doesn't end with his death on the cross. Three days later, the Gospels tell us, he was resurrected and appeared to his disciples. Thus, a skeptic might be tempted to ask: Did Jesus really *die* on the cross? Could he have survived and, perhaps, faked a resurrection? An interesting question—but modern medicine has shown any claim that Jesus survived his execution to lack credibility. Remember that Jesus was not only crucified—he was also brutally scourged prior to being handed his cross.

In 1986, a team of medical experts set out to define the physiological consequences of Jesus' scourging and crucifixion. Their conclusions, published in the *Journal of the American Medical Association,* leave no room for Jesus to have survived his ordeal. Regarding scourging, the researchers write: "The usual instrument was a short whip . . . with several single or braided leather thongs of variable lengths, in which [were] small iron balls or sharp pieces of sheep bones. . . . The scourging . . . was intended to weaken the victim to a state just short of collapse or death." They also note:

> As the Roman soldiers repeatedly struck the victim's back with full force, the iron balls would cause deep contusions, and the leather thongs and sheep bones would cut into the skin and subcutaneous tissues. Then, as the flogging continued, the lacerations would tear into the underlying skeletal muscles and produce quivering ribbons of bleeding flesh.[160]

In the abstract they affirm: "The scourging produced deep stripelike lacerations and appreciable blood loss, and it probably set the stage for hypovolemic shock, as evidenced by the fact that Jesus was too weakened to carry the crossbar to Golgotha." This leads them to their conclusion: "Modern medical interpretation of the historical evidence indicates that Jesus was dead when taken down from the cross." So even *before* he set foot on Calvary to be crucified, it's very possible that Jesus was already nearing death due to shock, dehydration, and blood loss.

Consider Jesus' likely physiological state by the time he was taken down from the cross by Joseph of Arimathea. Over the preceding hours he had suffered extreme blood loss, shock, dehydration, internal bleeding, soft-tissue damage, extreme fatigue, nails through the extremities, a pierced heart, a pierced lung, and near-asphyxiation. Furthermore, the Roman soldiers who crucified Jesus and pierced his side were professional executioners: they knew how to get the job done. Death for a victim like Jesus would be certain *short of a miracle.*

Anastasis

Manifestations of the miraculous have always been a part of the Christian story. Even a skim through the pages of the New Testament will reveal numerous miracles associated with Jesus' ministry. But although these events occurred long ago, there are good reasons to believe that miracles are not only things of the distant past.

The skeptical philosopher David Hume believed that miracles were unreasonable to believe because they go against the laws of nature, and are thus incompatible with uniform human experience. Notable theologian Craig Keener begs to differ, and has accordingly assembled a massive two-volume scholarly work demonstrating that miraculous experiences continue to be reported in colossal numbers—he has confirmed "hundreds of millions" of miracle claims—all over the world.[161] Of course, human testimony itself does not prove beyond doubt that supernatural signs and wonders have occurred. But all it takes is one—*one* miracle to prove the existence of the supernatural. Could all the hundreds of millions of reports confirmed by Keener be dubious? For one thing, this would take a massive amount of case-by-case research. There is nothing irrational about the concept of a miracle. If God exists and is acting in the world he created, then there is no reason he couldn't suspend the laws of nature for his purposes. God sustains the world in being just as a train engine sustains a boxcar in motion, and so by virtue of his "closeness" to natural things he grounds in being, he can easily manipulate their behavior, just as an engine can manipulate the motion of a boxcar. Or think of it this way: a three-year-old cannot ordinarily walk on water—unless an outside agent (say, his father) lifts him and moves him along the surface of the water. His father has the power to help his three-year-old do something that he, otherwise, could not do.

This is how God works when it comes to the miraculous: he willfully unites his power to created things, enabling them to behave in ways they otherwise might not. God doesn't *break* the laws of nature, because he *makes* the laws of nature, which he does by creating and sustaining things that will act in predictable, ordered ways according to their natures; that is, according to what they *are*. For this reason, we might think of the laws of nature as "the laws of *natures*" which are just descriptions of how things normally behave—behavior which God, as creator of those natures, can alter as he sees fit.

This brings us to the central miracle of Christianity: the resurrection of Jesus Christ. The New Testament writers profess it happened, some even claiming to have seen the risen Lord with their own eyes. Consider the ancient Christian creed in Paul's first letter to the Corinthians:

> For I delivered to you of first importance what I also received, that Christ died for our sins in accordance with the scriptures, that he was buried, that he was raised on the third day in accordance with the scriptures, and that he appeared to Cephas, then to the twelve. Then he appeared to more than five hundred brethren at one time, most of whom are still alive, though some have fallen asleep. Then he appeared to James, then to all the apostles. Last of all, as to one untimely born, he appeared also to me (1 Cor. 15:3–8).

Paul tells us two very important things: (1) that the disciples believed Jesus had appeared to them after the Crucifixion, and (2) that Paul himself, a former persecutor of Christians, was converted after an encounter with the resurrected Jesus. Both things, like the Crucifixion, are among Habermas's "minimal facts" recognized by Christian and non-Christian historians alike. Skeptic Paula Fredriksen of Boston University admits: "I know in their own terms what they saw was the raised Jesus. . . . I'm not saying that they really did see the raised Jesus. I wasn't there. I don't know what they saw. But I do know as a historian that they must have seen something."[162]

Consider the apostles before the Resurrection. They were simple and "uneducated" men (Acts 4:13), many of them fishermen. They also seem to have been somewhat passive and even cowardly, as indicated by their abandonment of Jesus after his arrest and their tendency to hide after his crucifixion. And who could forget Peter's threefold denial of Jesus? Yet even the disciples—like their persecutor Paul—seemed to undergo *an immediate and radical shift in character* in the days after the death of Christ. The best explanation for this is that they had encountered what they truly believed to be the resurrected Christ.

Early Church writers confirm that the apostles suffered greatly for proclaiming the gospel. To escape persecution and death, all they had to do was deny the resurrection of Christ. But they held firm to what they believed—to what they had heard, seen, and even touched—and tradition tells us that most of them paid the ultimate price for it, not just being tortured but eventually losing their lives. To the apostles and the other ancient Christian martyrs, this life was nothing compared to what was to come. Death was welcomed because, to these men and women, eternal life in heaven was the one that mattered.

Unless there was a true resurrection of Jesus—unless the early Christians were really convinced that Jesus had really been raised from the dead—there is no way to explain Christianity's sudden and unexpected rise from non-proselytizing Judaism. As N.T. Wright put it, "I cannot explain the rise of early Christianity unless Jesus rose again, leaving an empty tomb behind him."[163]

Of course, skeptics offer alternative explanations for why the apostles and disciples believed they had seen the resurrected

Christ. One of the most popular explanations is *hallucination*. Did Peter, Mary Magdalene, and the others see and experience a risen Jesus who wasn't there? It's possible: grief-induced hallucinations are known to occur. But grief-induced *mass* hallucinations are not. Recall that Jesus appeared to the disciples both individually *and in groups*. In fact, Paul recalls in his first letter to the Corinthians that the resurrected Christ "appeared to more than five hundred brethren at one time, most of whom are still alive" (1 Cor. 15:3–7). So not only did Jesus appear after his death to five hundred people at once, but some of these witnesses were still alive when Paul wrote this. He's essentially saying to the people in Corinth, "Go ask these people for yourself if you don't believe me!"

There is another problem with the hallucination theory: Paul's conversion. Remember that Paul, when he was still Saul of Tarsus, was a vicious persecutor of Christians. The likelihood of him grieving over the death of Jesus to the point of hallucination is nil. Paul's notorious pre-Christian reputation as a persecutor is attested by multiple sources. So is his conversion, which is why nearly all New Testament scholars accept it as another one of Habermas's minimal facts. What caused such a radical change of heart and mind in Paul? According to Luke, and Paul himself, it was an encounter with the risen Jesus.[164]

Now there is an important distinction to be made here. To the first-century Jew the word "resurrection" did not mean mere survival; nor did it mean physical resuscitation. Resurrection (Greek, *anastasis*) meant "life after death."[165] This is what the disciples proclaimed about their divine Messiah after the crucifixion; *this* was the gospel—that Jesus had been resurrected bodily from the dead.

But the Resurrection was not where the story ended. The early Christians saw themselves not just as "brothers and sisters" but "sons and daughters" of the same Almighty Father. They were filled with the same Holy Spirit, and worshipped one and the same savior, Jesus Christ. They were the Church. As history moved forward, the Church continued to grow with mysterious persistence, and Christians continued to die for their faith; with each one who was martyred, new ones would rise up. And so it continued through the centuries, as they persisted in its divine mission through war, persecution, corruption, heresy, and scandal. What mere earthly institution could have survived such challenges, century after century? Only, I am convinced, an indestructible one empowered and fortified by God.

Catholicism should be taken seriously whether one believes in it or not. For there are good reasons to believe that it is the original and most authentic form of Christianity. Moreover, its founder claimed to be God and people *believed* him, making him the most influential person to have ever lived. Its sacred text is more widely read than any other, or any work of fiction or nonfiction in history. Despite persecution and increasing secularization, it remains the largest religion in the world and continues to spread. Its influence on Western civilization and culture is incomparable. And though its leaders throughout its history have included many scoundrels, the Catholic Church has also produced the best people who have ever lived—the saints.

With all that in mind, can someone be justified in being indifferent toward the Catholic faith and the Catholic Church? Not if there are good reasons to believe that it is the *one* true faith and the *one* true Church founded by Jesus Christ. And I think there are—as we will see in Part III.

Why Worship in the Catholic Church?

We do not really need a religion that is right where we are right. What we need is a religion that is right where we are wrong.

—G.K. Chesterton, *The Catholic Church and Conversion*

9

Authority and the Catholic Church

My reconversion to the Catholic Church did not occur all at once. After reluctantly attending a weekend retreat at which I had been invited to assist with the music, I found myself unexpectedly moved by the experience. My plan going into the retreat was to do my part with the band, and when it was time for the spiritual stuff—the prayer, the talks, the small group sessions—I would hide in the shadows. I did not feel like I belonged there.

Yet there I was. And the spiritual stuff I had every intention of avoiding that weekend caught me by surprise; by the second evening I felt a strong pull toward the confessional. As an adult, I had never made a thorough, sincere confession to a priest. I had either obscured the gravity of my wrongdoings with vague, euphemistic language—or I had omitted them altogether. That night I made a good, honest confession and something was restored to my being that I can only describe as "Light." Although I was in the presence of a priest I sensed nothing but the presence of Christ himself. He was as palpably present to me as my own heartbeat. Then and there, and in the moments of prayer and surrender afterward, I felt my heart not merely changing, but being re*newed*.

That initial conversion—my "conversion of heart"—was primarily emotional. But my "conversion of mind" was more complex and took much longer. I had many questions and objections still to deal with. The turning point for me was when I discovered St. John Paul the Great's teachings on human sexuality, his Theology of the Body. For the first time in my life I had sought to discover why the Church teaches what it does about contraception, abortion, divorce, and other such issues; and I was astonished at the clarity and subtlety of those teachings. It was evident, in the light of Revelation and Sacred Tradition, and with the guidance of the Holy Spirit, that the Church had thought these issues through very carefully and thoroughly. Finally it all made sense to me. "If the Church can get it right on *these* issues," I thought to myself, "then I should have little doubt about the rest being reasonable as well." Thus began a newfound confidence that the Catholic Church is the one, true Church of God—what St. Paul calls the "pillar and foundation of truth" (1 Tim. 3:15).

Authority matters

One of the most challenging aspects of conversion to Catholicism is checking one's ego and trusting the Church's judgment on matters of faith and morals, especially when our understanding is incomplete. Antitheists like to caricature religious faith as blind, but it really is no more so than, say, a student's trust in his professor. He accepts his professor's teachings, but not blindly or credulously: he seeks deeper understanding and confirmation of his beliefs. This is exactly what religious believers do (or should do). The Catholic Church reverences human reason and has nothing to hide; it therefore imposes no restrictions on asking questions and examining the Faith critically, provided the inquiry is an honest pursuit of truth and understanding. In the end, of course, Catholics are expected to trust the Church's judgment more than their own, which follows logically from accepting that the Church is guided into all truth by the Holy Spirit.

Very fitting is St. Anselm's phrase: *fides quaerens intellectum*—"faith seeking understanding." Faith is not static; it is active and vibrant, and perfected by understanding. Further, it is not merely intellectual, but is energized by charity. Without charity, faith is barren and ineffectual. As Paul explained it: faith works itself out in love, and without love it amounts to nothing (Gal. 5:6; 1 Cor. 13:2). A child obeys his father because he trusts that his father "knows better" and has his best interests in mind. The same applies for Christians who love Christ. And because the Church and Christ are one, to obey the Church is to obey Christ; and to disobey the Church . . . well, you get the point. This theology of the identity of Christ with his Church goes all the way back to the road to Damascus, where Jesus asked Saul of Tarsus, "Saul, Saul, why do you persecute *me*?" After Saul became the apostle Paul, he developed this theology in his epistles.[166] It was further developed and affirmed in subsequent centuries, as when Aquinas wrote in his *Summa*, "Head and members form as it were one and the same mystical person" (ST III:48:2);[167] and when St. Joan of Arc famously declared: "About Jesus Christ and the Church, I simply know they're just one thing, and we shouldn't complicate the matter."

The "obedience of faith," as Paul called it, is central to the Catholic life (Rom. 1:5, 16:26). Catholics believe that the Church teaches with the authority of Christ. Every bishop of the Catholic Church has been ordained in a line of direct succession from the apostles; they are the official guardians of Church teaching. Catholics therefore hold that the teaching office of bishop carries the authority of Christ: "He who hears you hears me," assured the Lord (Luke 10:16). It follows, then, that *every* teaching of the Church should be accepted with faithful obedience. Aquinas explains why:

> He who adheres to the teaching of the Church, as to an infallible rule, assents to whatever the Church teaches; otherwise, if, of the things taught by the Church, he holds what he chooses to hold, and rejects what he chooses to reject, he no longer adheres to the teaching of the Church as to an infallible rule, but to his own will. . . . Therefore it is clear that such a [person who refuses to be corrected by the Church] with regard to one article has no faith in the other articles, but only a kind of opinion in accordance with his own will (ST II:5:3).

It should be surprising, then, to say that one of the most difficult aspects of converting to the Catholic faith is conforming one's life to Church teachings—whether one fully understands them, or likes them, or not. Indeed, man has been allergic to authority since the Garden of Eden. But as faith deepens and matures, this submission becomes much easier.

Clearly the prospect of having to submit to the authority of the Church (especially in moral matters) could be a barrier to anyone contemplating conversion, especially in our permissive and radically individualistic culture. That this suspicion of authority leads to religious indifferentism, there can be no doubt. Those steeped in the culture of "me" or "meh" (take your pick) want to remain masters of their world, unwittingly becoming slaves to themselves—or even something worse.

Individualism and Christianity

An excessive sense of self-sufficiency breeds an unhealthy contempt of authority. Teenagers are a case in point. I remember quite clearly what it was like to be a teen under my parents' roof; and although we dwelled in peace most days, there were occasional disputes—instigated by me—when I believed I knew better than they. I especially remember our disputes about how late I could stay out at night, my parents usually imposing a before-midnight curfew while I stubbornly argued for an after-midnight one. They understood, however, that the saying "nothing good happens after midnight" was not merely a cliché. Looking back, I can clearly see the wisdom behind their rules and restrictions; but at the time I couldn't, blinded by my self-centeredness.

In her essay "The Lost Tools of Learning," Dorothy Sayers calls the onset of adolescence "the Poetic age." She explains: "It is self-centered; it yearns to express itself; it rather specializes in being misunderstood; it is restless and tries to achieve independence." The adolescent experiences a particularly acute existential desire to live for himself while relying very little on others. The hot rush of individualistic fervor courses through the veins.

It seems that we as a culture are living in a Poetic Age now—exalting individualism and obsessing over our own self-expression. We rely on ourselves—and our devices—more and more, and on other people less and less. No wonder, then, that researchers have noticed a trend toward prolonged adolescence. According to Columbia University psychiatrist Mirjana Domakonda,

"Twenty-five is the new 18, and delayed adolescence is no longer a theory, but a reality. In some ways, we're all in a 'psychosocial moratorium,' experimenting with a society where swipes constitute dating and likes are the equivalent of conversation."[168] It is not surprising that such an intellectually stagnant, self-absorbed culture would be uninterested in religious authority, dogma, and community.

Individualism has also had an impact on Christendom itself. The Protestant Reformation is probably the most significant example. In the sixteenth century, the Reformers swung the door open to private interpretation of Scripture and the false doctrine of *sola scriptura* ("Scripture alone") by renouncing the Church's teaching authority. The result was doctrinal chaos—a situation of "every man his own pope"—and the destruction of Christian unity.

As one man disagreed with another's personal interpretation of Scripture, new Protestant communities were formed. What followed was a ceaseless proliferation of denominations—Lutheran, Anabaptist, Calvinist, Anglican, Wesleyan, Baptist, and eventually other splinter sects. The Catholic Church itself came to be seen as just one of many denominations. Disagreement often turned to violence, with both Catholics and Protestants at fault. The scandal of this violence was a major factor in the rise of the Enlightenment.

It cannot be denied that the sixteenth-century Catholic Church needed reformation, perhaps even desperately. Indeed, inasmuch as its human element comprises sinful men and women, the Church will *always* need reformation. But although the Protestant Reformers may have gotten some things right about the problems in the Church, they were glaringly wrong in their solutions. As historian Steve Weidenkopf has pointed out, what we call the Protestant Reformation was something more akin to a *revolution*:

> Any movement that seeks to destroy the Church—its organization, its sacraments, its way of life—and replace it with something new and not in conformity with apostolic tradition and history is a revolution, not a reformation.[169]

The Reformers' strict emphasis on personal interpretation of Scripture, coupled with their rejection of the guiding authority of the apostolic Church, led inevitably to a proliferative Protestant revolution, and a scandalous dividing of Christendom into thousands of denominations. The Church had experienced division in previous centuries, but this was something altogether worse. The Catholic writer Hilaire Belloc was unsparing in his assessment of the Protestant revolt's consequences, writing in his 1936 book *Characters of the Reformation*: "The break-up of united western Christendom with the coming of the Reformation was by far the most important thing in history since the formation of the Catholic Church fifteen hundred years before."[170]

What Protestantism cannot offer

I have never met an insincere Protestant. If I have, either I don't recall it or I was fooled. But as far as I can tell, every Protestant I've ever encountered has believed with all sincerity that Jesus Christ is truly the Lord and Savior of all; and that the Catholic Church is *not* the Church founded by Christ. It is not hard to find a Protestant who was once Catholic; nor is it hard to find a Catholic who was once Protestant. But I have noticed a distinct difference between the two. Often Catholic-to-Protestant converts seem to have an emotional discontentment, if not an abiding contempt, for their former Catholic faith. On the other hand, Protestant-to-Catholic converts seem consistently to be grateful for their Protestant experience (in fact I have never met one who felt otherwise). Why might this be?

Protestantism has much to offer to those who are seeking God, by encouraging a personal relationship with Jesus Christ and trust in Holy Scripture as a guide for daily living. Finally, Protestantism offers opportunities for worship and emphasizes Christian brotherhood.

The Catholic Church shares these values. But if we are being honest, it may seem that many Protestant churches have more on offer—especially when it comes to emotional engagement and a communal experience—than the typical Catholic parish. Indeed, many Protestant churches, especially of the Evangelical denominations, can boast of hip pastors, lively music, gripping sermons, extensive opportunities for Bible study, free babysitting services on Sunday mornings, and overall just more religious enthusiasm.

But although some Protestant churches may offer more in terms of emotional and social *experience*—the Catholic Church offers something much deeper. There is a degree of spiritual engagement possible in the Catholic Church that is unattainable outside of it, a participation in a threefold unity: unity in truth, unity in Christ, and unity as Church; or to put it another way, unity in doctrine, unity through sacrament, and unity within the communion of the saints.

10

Union in Truth

My two good pals, John and Luke, are Evangelical Christians. When the three of us get together, suffice it to say that there are no elephants in the room; both guys usually have a Catholic joke or two to offer in my direction. Of course, this jesting is in good fun and comes from a place of brotherly affection. But although we acknowledge our denominational differences with good humor, we spend far more time talking seriously about our religious convictions, our reasons for believing—or rejecting— certain doctrines and religious practices.

John was raised in a Lutheran home and was baptized as an infant, as I was. Though our views of baptism diverge in some respects, he believes that infant baptism is permissible, and analogous to the Old Testament practice of circumcising a Jewish child into the covenant. Luke, on the other hand, was baptized as an adult and is not convinced that infant baptism is doctrinally sound.

Imagine that Luke, John, and I each wrote down our different theological view of baptism. Some of the differences would be subtle, but others glaring. I wonder what would happen if we were able to send these summaries back in time to St. Peter and ask him which view best fits *his* theology; remember: he is the one who wrote, "Baptism . . . now saves us" (1 Pet. 31), and preached on Pentecost, "Repent, and be baptized every one of you in the name of Jesus Christ for the forgiveness of your sins . . . For the promise is to you and to your children" (Acts 2:38–39). Imagine further what, say, Irenaeus of Lyons would say about our views on baptism in the second century; or Cyprian of Carthage in the third; or Augustine of Hippo in the fourth. Fortunately, we know exactly what these men thought about baptism from their writings. Augustine, for example, wrote the following:

"There are three ways in which sins are forgiven: in baptism, in prayer, and in the greater humility of penance; yet God does not forgive sins except to the baptized."[171]

If Luke, John, and I wanted to explore our other doctrinal differences we could write down our beliefs about, say, the Lord's Supper, then Purgatory, then Mary. At the end of the day we would be able to establish two facts: first, that our understandings of doctrine are contradictory; second, that the doctrines of the Catholic Church today are strikingly and completely compatible with the doctrines of the early Church, whereas the core Protestant doctrines of *sola scriptura* and *sola fide* are not.

The Catholic Church, as the "pillar and foundation of truth" (1 Tim. 3:15), understands its whole body of definitive teaching to be free of error. Protestant denominations affirm many of the same truths as Catholics; but by virtue of their *protest* against core beliefs and practices passed on by the apostles to their successors, they do not possess and proclaim the fullness of "the faith which was once for all delivered to the saints" (Jude 3). This is why Catholics evangelize Protestants: they want their non-Catholic brothers and sisters to accept *all* of what the Church teaches. Protestant-to-Catholic conversion, in other words, does not involve deletion so much as it involves completion.

Where should Christians get their doctrine from?

At the end of Matthew's Gospel, when the resurrected Jesus commissions his disciples to go and make disciples of all nations, he does not say "teach them to observe *some* of what I have commanded you" or "*most* of what I have commanded." Here is what he does say:

All authority in heaven and on earth has been given to me. Go therefore and make disciples of all nations, baptizing them in the name of the Father and of the Son and of the Holy Spirit, teaching them to observe *all* that I have commanded you; and lo, I am with you always, to the close of the age (Matt. 28:16–20).

Jesus was not interested in telling people what they wanted to hear at the expense of truth. He was interested in orthodoxy or *right teaching*. "Our Lord Christ has surnamed himself Truth, not Custom," wrote Tertullian. For Jesus and his apostles there was no room in the Church for false teachings; and especially no room for *indifference* to false teachings. For that reason the great minds of the Catholic Church have always taken the development of doctrine very seriously, always refining its formulations and drawing logical conclusions from the deposit of apostolic teaching with great care. The pool of doctrine from which it draws is deep, having developed in much the same way a newborn develops into an adult. Or as Bishop Robert Barron writes, the truth of the Church "is not so much like a football, dumbly passed from generation to generation, but much more like a winding river or a luxuriant tree, ever sending off new shoots and branches."[172]

Bishop Barron writes this in his foreword to John Cardinal Henry Newman's classic study *An Essay on the Development of Christian Doctrine*. Indeed, there is no one who has written more eloquently on this topic than Newman, who began writing his *Essay* as a Protestant and finished it as a Catholic. His conversion from Anglicanism resulted from his research involving the writings of the early Church Fathers. There he discovered their devotion to apostolic doctrines that were unmistakeably Catholic, in their most primitive forms and even more so in its maturing forms, leading Newman to conclude: "Modern Catholicism is nothing else but simply the legitimate growth and complement, that is, the natural and necessary development, of the doctrine of the early Church." Thus, he wrote famously, "To be deep in history is to cease to be Protestant."

Newman drew another important conclusion from his research: if apostolic doctrine was to develop organically over time, an *infallible* authority would be needed to ensure that developments remained orthodox. Only Rome had ever claimed or exercised such an interpretative authority, in the Church's Magisterium as constituted by the pope and the bishops teaching in union with him.

Some non-Catholics prefer what is almost an anti-dogmatism. They fear doctrinal controversies to be a hindrance to a personal relationship with God, creating a false "head or heart" dilemma. But Catholics and other more doctrinally interested denominations see doctrine and relationship as a congenial combination. In the first place, on a purely natural level, doctrine is unavoidable for every thinking creature. It is doctrinal even to say there is no doctrine, which of course is self-refuting. More importantly, the head and the heart are cooperative because you cannot love what you don't know, and the more you know about it the more fully you can love it. Therefore, as Frank Sheed taught us, the more you know about God, the more you can love about God. We are, after all, charged by Scripture to love God with all our heart, *mind*, soul, and strength. So doctrine—in fact—is a very good thing because it expands the horizons of love and, by extension, one's relationship with God. The head is at the service of the heart.

As we have already noted, orthodoxy amounts to *true teaching* about reality; and true teaching leads to true knowledge. If you don't have true teaching regarding Christ and his Church then you can't properly love Christ and his Church, because (it is worth repeating) you can't love what you don't know. In fact, for St. Paul, getting doctrine right is not just a matter of truth but a matter of *salvation*: "Watch your life and doctrine closely," he exhorts, "Persevere in them, because if you do, you will save both yourself and your hearers" (1 Tim. 4:16, NIV). Thus, every Christian ought to test everything, continually seeking a fuller knowledge of the truth, and holding fast to what is true. He has an obligation (at least according to Paul) to avoid being "tossed to and fro . . . carried about with every wind of doctrine, by the cunning of men" (Gal. 4:14). Indifference is not an option from the biblical standpoint—not in a religion where seeking and loving the truth is central, and especially where the truth being sought is in fact a Person infinitely knowable (John 14:6).

Of course, most Christians are going to agree on some fundamental doctrines: that God became man; that God is one divine nature in three persons; that the Bible is the inspired word of God; that a personal relationship with God is paramount to the Christian life. But on the question of authority, things get foggy. The Catholic claim is that Christ founded a Church with a threefold authority: Sacred Scripture, Sacred Tradition, and the Magisterium (the living teaching authority of the Church consisting of the pope and bishops). Indeed, the Magisterium serves the word of God—which has been passed down orally (Tradition) and by letter (the Bible)—as her interpreter and guardian (2 Thess. 2:15; Matt. 16:15–20; 18:18). The Church is therefore the authoritative confirmer and communicator of Christian doctrine on earth.

I am certain that if non-Catholics saw the Catholic Church *as it really is*, many would enter it at any cost, not merely as a change of denomination but as the perfection—a completion—of the faith they have held all along. If the Catholic Church really is "the household of God, built upon the foundation of the apostles and prophets" and the "pillar and foundation of the truth" (Eph. 2:20, 1 Tim. 3:15), then what Christian would not want to be *in it*? The innumerable denominations that make up Protestantism cannot be "the Church" founded by Christ for they are wracked by contradictions, and truth does not contradict itself. The true Church must be unified and profess a single set of beliefs that can be traced back to the apostles. In other words, it must be *doctrinally sound* and similar *in structure* to the Church of the New Testament. The question is: does the Catholic Church best match the early Church in both doctrine and structure?

The first Christians

For another thought experiment, imagine that a Catholic deacon, a Southern Baptist minister, and a nondenominational "megachurch" pastor travel back in time to the second century to worship with the early Christians. Now ask yourself who would be more comfortable in the worship service: *who would be more at home?* To answer this, we might consider St. Justin Martyr's description in his *First Apology* of a second-century liturgy:

But we, after we have thus washed him who has been convinced and has assented to our teaching, bring him to the place where those who are called brethren are assembled, in order that we may offer hearty prayers in common for ourselves and for the baptized person, and for all others in every place [*the Prayers of the Faithful*], that we may be . . . found good citizens and keepers of the commandments, so that we may be saved with an everlasting salvation.

Having ended the prayers, we salute one another with a kiss [*the Sign of Peace*]. There is then brought to the president of the brethren bread and a cup of wine mixed with water; and he taking them, gives praise and glory to the Father of the universe, through the name of the Son and of the Holy Ghost, and offers thanks at considerable length for our being counted worthy to receive these things at his hands. And when he has concluded the prayers and thanksgivings [*the Eucharistic Prayer*], all the people present express their assent by saying Amen [*the Great Amen*]. This word Amen answers in the Hebrew language to γένοιτο [so be it].

And when the president has given thanks, and all the people have expressed their assent, those who are called by us deacons give to each of those present to partake of the bread and wine mixed with water over which the thanksgiving was pronounced, and to those who are absent they carry away a portion.[173]

Justin wrote these words around A.D. 155. Notice the parts of the ancient liturgy still present in the Catholic Mass of today (italicized above in square brackets): the Prayers of the Faithful, the Sign of Peace, the Eucharistic Prayer, and the Great Amen. Notice also, in the first paragraph, that salvation in the *final* sense is not taken for granted, but instead depends on one's perseverance in charity and obedience to God's commandments "so that we may be saved." Finally, notice that a priest ("president") and deacon fulfill specific roles in the Eucharistic liturgy. It is also worth noting what Justin says about the sacraments of baptism and the Eucharist in the next paragraph:

And this food is called among us Εὐχαριστία [the Eucharist], of which no one is allowed to partake but the man who believes that the things which we teach are true, and who has been washed with the washing that is for the remission of sins, and unto regeneration, and who is so living as Christ has enjoined. For not as common bread and common drink do we receive these; but in like manner as Jesus Christ our savior, having been made flesh by the Word of God, had both flesh and blood for our salvation, so likewise have we been taught that the food which is blessed by the prayer of his word, and from which our blood and flesh by transmutation are nourished, is the flesh and blood of that Jesus who was made flesh.[174]

Clearly, the Catholic deacon would be the most comfortable of our three time-traveling Christians. Catholic philosopher Peter Kreeft conducted a similar imaginative exercise on himself when he was a young Calvinist. He immersed himself in the early Church writings and discovered that the earliest Church was unmistakeably Catholic in doctrine and in structure, though primitively so. He responded according to what he discovered—convenient or not—and became Catholic. Now a philosophy professor at Boston College, he is one of the Church's most esteemed apologists, respected by Catholics and Protestants alike.

Time travel not being an option, we should be thankful for the abundance of early Christian manuscripts and writings that testify to what the Church has always taught and practiced. In my experience, most Christians (Catholics included) have never even *thought* about reading early extra-biblical writings. Discovering the writings of the early Fathers was a game-changer for me, as it has been for many others. C.S. Lewis once remarked, "A young man who wishes to remain a sound Atheist cannot be too careful of his reading." Neither can a committed Protestant (as Cardinal Newman found out).

The writings of the early Church Fathers have been for many non-Catholics the deciding factor in their conversion to

Catholicism. Not only do these ancient sources reveal the nature of the early Church and her teachings, but they shed light on those "elusive" biblical texts in support of Catholic doctrine that have been contemplated and appreciated throughout the ages. Marcus Grodi, a former Evangelical pastor as well as founder and president of The Coming Home Network International, writes: "Certainly an amazing majority of converts mention how reading the early Church Fathers, either for the first time or for the first time with awareness, convinced them that the early Church was amazingly Catholic and certainly not Protestant!"[175]

The word *catholic* means "according to the whole" or more simply "universal". That is what it has always meant in a Christian context: that there is one Church of the one God of the universe, and everyone is invited to be a member. The word became an upper-cased proper noun, "Catholic," when other Christian bodies began to oppose the Church. The earliest use of the term in its original adjectival form is in a second-century letter of St. Ignatius of Antioch: "Wherever the bishop shall appear, there let the multitude of the people also be; even as wherever Jesus Christ is, there is the catholic Church."[176] Ignatius does not explain what "catholic" means, suggesting that it was already a familiar term in the Church community.

Ignatius also refers to the bishop as the leader of the people: "Wherever the bishop shall appear, there let the multitude of the people also be." The hierarchical ranks in the Church conferred by the sacrament of holy orders—bishop, priest and deacon—were a prominent aspect of the early Church, as they remain today. Anyone who reads the Acts of the Apostles and the epistles of Paul (especially to Timothy and Titus) will discover a clear hierarchical structure in the early Church after Christ. In A.D. 110, shortly after the New Testament was written, Ignatius writes in his letter to the Magnesians:

> Take care to do all things in harmony with God, with the *bishop* presiding in the place of God, and with the *presbyters* [priests] in the place of the council of the apostles, and

with the *deacons*, who are most dear to me, entrusted with the business of Jesus Christ.[177]

Furthermore, Christ required that there be a succession of his apostles until the end of the age, and this *apostolic succession* continues today. Every bishop in today's Catholic Church has been ordained in a direct line from the original twelve apostles of Christ. This has its roots in the Bible itself: at the beginning of the Acts of the Apostles, Peter stands up and recognizes that the office of Judas Iscariot has not yet been filled since his death. "His office let another take," declares Peter, quoting the book of Psalms; and Matthias is chosen to succeed Judas (Acts 1:15–26). Thus St. Clement of Rome, one of the first successors of St. Peter, wrote around A.D. 80:

> Our apostles knew through our Lord Jesus Christ that there would be strife for the office of bishop. For this reason, therefore, having received perfect foreknowledge, they appointed those who have already been mentioned and afterwards added the further provision that, *if they should die, other approved men should succeed to their ministry.*[178]

Peter and "the keys"

Man is an expert self-deceiver. As Chesterton mused, "a man's soul is as full of voices as a forest . . . fancies, follies, memories, madnesses, mysterious fears, and more mysterious hopes. All settlement and sane government of life consists in coming to the conclusion that some of those voices have authority and others not."[179] Similarly, the prophet Jeremiah wrote that "the heart is deceitful above all things, and desperately corrupt" (Jer. 17:9).

Although our tendency toward diversion and self-deception may be a cause of religious indifferentism, it could also be said that such tendencies most justify the necessity of true, organized religion—and divine revelation. Our inherent brokenness is why no organization can thrive without a clear voice of authority. It is almost painful to imagine a world without the likes of police, principals, mayors, presidents, prime ministers, pastors, and parents. We don't always love to be told what to do but, the Lord knows, we often need it.

Christendom, unfortunately, is full of many contradictory voices. For this reason the Christian must determine which voices have God-given authority and which do not. Then and only then will Christians be of one mind in doctrine and of one heart in worship. Then and only then can Christians have every means to become holy. If there *are* men who possess God-given authority within the Church, then every Christian ought to make it their first priority to determine where such men are to be found. Not only does divine revelation and the testimony of the early Church reveal a hierarchy of offices instituted by Christ, but a Church without such a hierarchy is an absurdity, given man's fallen nature. No Church can be a "pillar and bulwark of truth" without an infallible authority in matters of faith and morals guiding and overseeing it. Simply put, if the Church is what it claims to be, it needs a pope. Christ, is, of course, our heavenly king. But when the king is not in town, he always designates a prime minister—and perhaps secondary ministers—to rule in his stead. This is why Jesus established Peter as the chief apostle and made the papacy a necessary mark of the Church until he comes again.

In the Davidic kingdom of the Old Testament, the king had a right-hand man called his steward, who would exercise authority in the king's absence. As a sign of the authority the steward had conditionally been granted, he held the "keys" of the kingdom. Jesus makes a direct parallel to this: in Isaiah we read, "And I will place on [the steward's] shoulder the key of the house of David"; and Jesus says, "I will give you the keys of the kingdom of heaven." Isaiah says, "He shall open, and none shall shut; and he shall shut, and none shall open"; and Jesus says, "Whatever you bind on earth shall be bound in heaven, and whatever you loose on earth shall be loosed in heaven." The parallels are unmistakeable. Jesus is making Peter his "steward."

"Binding and loosing" is a first-century rabbinical term for "forbidding and permitting." For the early Christians, therefore, whoever has the authority to bind and loose has the authority to make decisions about Church doctrine and discipline. Jesus confers this authority on his apostles collectively, when he says, "Receive the Holy Spirit. If you forgive the sins of any, they are forgiven; if you retain the sins of any, they are retained" (John 20:22–23).[180] But the only *individual* apostle to whom Jesus speaks about binding and loosing is Peter: "I will give you [singular] the keys of the kingdom of heaven, and whatever you [singular] bind on earth shall be bound in heaven, and whatever you [singular] loose on earth shall be loosed in heaven" (Matt. 16:18).

So although the power to administrate is conferred upon the apostles as a group by Christ, the same power to govern is given in a unique way to Peter alone, the chief apostle. The Gospels show the primacy of Peter clearly. Every time the apostles are listed, Peter is the first to be mentioned (Matt 10:2; Luke 6:13–16; Acts 1:3). He is called the chief apostle (Matt. 10:2). He is among Jesus' inner three, and of them always the first mentioned (Matt. 17:1; Mark 5:37, 9:2, 14:33; Luke 8:51, 9:28). On several occasions, Peter is the only name mentioned among the group of disciples (Mark 16:7; 1 Cor. 9:5, 15:5; Acts 2:37). And his name (in the forms of Peter, Kepha and Cephas) is mentioned in the New Testament almost 200 times, whereas the next-most-mentioned apostle, John, is mentioned only about fifty times.

Another New Testament detail that suggests Peter's unique authority is Peter's dogmatic declaration regarding circumcision at the Council of Jerusalem, as narrated in the Acts of the Apostles. The atmosphere is thick with intense debate. The early Church leaders have gathered to decide whether Gentile converts to Christianity must be circumcised. Peter stands, and the boisterous apostles and elders immediately hush in deference to him. Then Peter delivers his conclusive decision on the matter—and nobody argues with him:

And after there had been much debate, Peter rose and said to them, "Brethren, you know that in the early days God made choice among you, that by my mouth the Gentiles should hear the word of the gospel and believe. . . . We believe that we shall be saved through the grace of the Lord Jesus, just as they will" (Acts 15:7–11).

Aligning with the New Testament, the early Church writers also recognized the special office entrusted to Peter and his successors. An early record of Peter's successors is provided by St. Irenaeus at the tail end of the second century.[181] From the beginning, it was understood that the bishop of Rome was the "chief" bishop—the one who held "the keys to the kingdom of heaven" (Matt. 16:18–20). St. Cyprian of Carthage writes in A.D. 251:

> Indeed, the others were also what Peter was [apostles], but a primacy is given to Peter, whereby it is made clear that there is but one Church and one chair. . . . If someone does not hold fast to this unity of Peter, can he imagine that he still holds the faith? If he [should] desert the chair of Peter upon whom the Church was built, can he still be confident that he is in the Church?[182]

Sir Arthur Conan Doyle, through his famed character Sherlock Holmes, wrote that it is insensible to "twist facts to suit theories, instead of theories to suit facts." The Catholic doctrine of the papacy fits the biblical and historical sources like a glove. Why then are so many Christians opposed to this ancient idea? One possibility is that they see the pope as a competitor for the authority of Scripture rather than its servant. Another is that they see the pope as a threat to their own private interpretations of the Bible. Whatever the answer (and there are undoubtedly many), the unique authority of the bishop of Rome, properly understood, is not a bad thing because it is a biblical thing. It is also a merciful thing, for it often sees what the corrupt heart of man—and especially the man without grace—cannot see (Pope

Paul VI's *Humanae Vitae* is a key example). It is therefore a gift to the people of God, though not only a blessing but a burden to Peter and his successors.

I doubt that Peter felt a rush of excitement when Jesus informed him that he would be the chief steward and possessor of the keys of the kingdom of heaven. If he said anything at all, it was likely something akin to, "Depart from me, for I am a sinful man, O Lord." And yet it is astonishing how God has been able to hold together his Church with one sinful man after another.

11

Union in Christ

One of the major functions of the Catholic Church is to provide the spiritual equipment that will enable believers to become the best version of themselves. In other words, the Church functions primarily to empower believers with the life of God—otherwise known as *grace*—so they can grow in virtue, and most particularly faith, hope, and love. This comes primarily through the sacraments, physical signs instituted by the Lord himself to give grace.

The sacraments, in fact, resemble the work of Christ in the Gospels, as he often conferred grace through physical things. One of the most striking examples is when Jesus heals the woman with the hemorrhage (Matt. 9:20–22; Mark 5:25–34; Luke 8:43–48). Here's the passage from Mark's Gospel:

> And there was a woman who had had a flow of blood for twelve years, and who had suffered much under many physicians, and had spent all that she had, and was no better but rather grew worse. She had heard the reports about Jesus, and came up behind him in the crowd and touched his garment. For she said, "If I touch even his garments, I shall be made well." And immediately the hemorrhage ceased; and she felt in her body that she was healed of her disease. And Jesus, perceiving in himself that power had gone forth from him, immediately turned about in the crowd, and said, "Who touched my garments?" . . . But the woman, knowing what had been done to her, came in fear and trembling and fell down before him, and told him the whole truth. And he said to her, "Daughter, your faith has made you well; go in peace, and be healed of your disease."

Here we find the three primary elements of a sacrament: first, physical thing for conferring grace; second, grace flowing from

God to the recipient; third, the recipient's faith. Catholic apologist Jimmy Akin explains:

> This passage contains all the elements of the sacramental principle: the woman's faith, the physical means (touching Jesus' clothes), and the supernatural power that went out from Jesus. When the woman came up to him and, with faith, touched his garment, the power of God was sent forth, and she was healed.[183]

Therefore, he concludes:

> This is how the sacraments work; God uses physical signs (water, oil, bread, wine, the laying on of hands) as vehicles for his grace, which we receive in faith.

Just as a picture can change your thoughts, so a sacrament can change your soul. To receive the sacraments has great spiritual consequence. It would be a serious error to see the sacraments as "optional" for the Christian, because they are the normative ways through which our Lord desired us to receive his grace. Certainly, a believer may receive the life of God into his soul in other ways: through prayer or good works, for example. But the *fullness* of grace that God wants to give is only available through the Catholic Church, particularly through these efficacious signs. The sacraments are meant to heal, to unite, to sanctify. Thus, a Christian who does not dispose himself to the sacraments of the Church, in the end, shortchanges himself of the totality of the gifts God wants him to have.

Incense, hymns, bread, wine, oil, stained-glass windows, statues: the Catholic Church intentionally makes an appeal to the *whole* person, body and spirit. Sacraments work on our senses and our spirit simultaneously, filling us literally with the life of God and changing us from the inside out. In religious terms, we are spiritually made pure and filled with supernatural life. In practical terms, our intellect is enlightened and our will is strengthened; the sacraments, inasmuch as they restore grace to the human person, are the antidotes to death, the penalty for rejecting God's friendship in the Garden of Eden. But these explanations are inadequate. Although mere words will always fail to definitively describe the goodness of God's gifts, some words come closer to portraying the sacramental reality than others.

The ultimate consequence of receiving God's life within us is, in fact, far beyond any consequence we could imagine, let alone speak. "The only-begotten Son of God, wanting to make us sharers in his divinity, assumed our nature, so that he, made man, might make men gods," wrote Aquinas, echoing the early Church Fathers (see CCC 460). He was only repeating what early Fathers of the Church, such as St. Athanasius, had affirmed hundreds of years earlier: that the Son of God became man so that we might become God. This is not to say that man's being will be dissolved into God and we as individuals will be no more; rather, we become more perfectly ourselves by becoming more perfectly united to Christ. Just as he showed Moses when he appeared to him as a burning bush, a bush ablaze but not consumed, God does not destroy us when we grow nearer. Being one with Christ in eternity completes God's project, as it were, of forming us in his image and likeness.

This idea of the divinization of man, or *theosis* as it is called in the Eastern tradition, is not mere metaphor. God really wants to make man like him in every way possible. Jesus was not kidding when he said, "be perfect as your Father in heaven is perfect" (Matt. 5:48). He was calling us to contemplate our future and to strive toward it with warrior-like tenacity. He was reminding us that our destiny is to be perfected in the image and likeness of God; we are to become what St. Peter called "partakers of the divine nature" (2 Peter 1:4). And all this is possible only because Jesus died for the life of the world. Jesus paid the price, and we get *life*—especially when we receive the sacraments, which were instituted for that purpose by Christ.

The total package

The sacraments are the total package for the Christian who is seriously striving for holiness.

Through baptism a person is spiritually born again; he is fed by the Eucharist; he is equipped by confirmation; he is healed through confession and the anointing of the sick; and finally through matrimony, holy orders, or another calling he receives his vocation, his "way" to heaven. The purpose of all the sacraments is to draw us deeper into a life of faith; that is, to make us into saints—holy men and women of God.

Catholics believe that it is through baptism that a person is born again into a new life with Christ. Without this divine life that is breathed into the soul by God at baptism, a person lacks the supernatural "equipment" needed to live in heaven (he is an astronaut without a space suit, figuratively speaking). Another name for that supernatural equipment is *grace*.

What about salvation through faith as St. Paul so clearly professes in his letters? Well, drawing especially from the letters of St. Paul, St. James, and the Gospels, Catholics believe that one is saved by grace (Eph. 2:8) through faith (Rom. 3:26) working in love (Gal. 5:6, 1 Cor. 13). Jesus makes it clear that faith without love is dead, because faith is animated by works of love. Without love, religious faith is unavailing.

So along with the unanimous testimony of the early Church Fathers, the sacrament of baptism is professed by Catholics to be the initial "work of love" that leads to salvation. Jesus told Nicodemus that unless he was born of water and spirit he could not enter the kingdom of heaven (John 3:5). In his first sermon to the Church, Peter preached, "Repent, and be baptized every one of you in the name of Jesus Christ for the forgiveness of your sins" (Acts 2:38). He is even more explicit in his first New Testament letter: "Baptism . . . now saves you" (1 Pet. 3:21). Confirming the tradition of the apostles, Tertullian writes at the turn of the third century, "Happy is our sacrament of water, in that, by washing away the sins of our early blindness, we are set free and admitted into eternal life."[184]

Baptism now saves us. It is our initial reception and renewal of grace but not necessarily our last. The world was redeemed once and for all through the death of Christ, but individual

salvation is a process of sanctification that demands perseverance; it is not a one-time event. That is why Paul can write that
"the word of the cross is folly to those who are perishing, *but to
us who are being saved* it is the power of God" (1 Cor. 1:18), and
why he warns in a spirit of humility, "I am not aware of anything
against myself, but I am not thereby acquitted. It is the Lord who
judges me. Therefore do not pronounce judgment before the
time, before the Lord comes" (1 Cor. 4:4–5).

Salvation is by grace. It is pure gift. That is why babies are not
excluded from baptism. On the other hand, every child who is
baptized will be required to say "yes" to Christ for themselves
once they have reached the age of reason (this is another purpose
of the sacrament of confirmation. From baptism onward, "salvation is worked out in fear and trembling" (Phil. 2:12) and "he
who endures to the end will be saved" (Matt. 10:22).

Although Christians are saved initially when they are baptized there is still the problem of sin. Thus, Jesus gave his
apostles the authority to forgive sins on his behalf *in the person
of Christ* (2 Cor. 2:10). Jesus said to the apostles, "Receive the
Holy Spirit. If you forgive the sins of any, they are forgiven; if
you retain the sins of any, they are retained" (John 20:21–23).
Paul refers to this as "the ministry of reconciliation" (2 Cor.
5:18). Such a sacrament is truly a gift to the people of God. As
Chesterton says: "When a Catholic comes from Confession,
he does truly, by definition, step out again into that dawn of
his own beginning and look with new eyes across the world.
. . . He is now a new experiment of the Creator. He is as
much a new experiment as he was when he was really only
five years old. . . . He may be grey and gouty; but he is only
five minutes old."

Confession of one's sins to a priest is a beautiful but not an
easy thing. Nonetheless, it is essential to every Christian's life,
and one's failure to put himself at the feet of Jesus in this sacrament can have eternal consequences. We have only this life to
confess our sins and obtain new life within us as a result. St.
Cyprian writes around 250 A.D:

I beseech you, brethren, let everyone who has sinned confess his sin while he is still in this world, while his confession is still admissible, while the satisfaction and remission made through the priests are still pleasing before the Lord.[185]

But we must be careful to avoid a consumerist understanding of Church. I am not urging that one should be in the Catholic Church so they can "get" grace and that's that. Rather, for the love of truth and, above all, the love of God, every Christian should *hunger* for the sacraments once they see them for what they really are.

Why go to Mass?

The Dominican friar Aidan Nichols has proposed that "the 're-enchantment' of the Catholic Liturgy" is the most urgent ecclesial need of our time.[186] It is difficult to see how he could be wrong, since the Eucharistic liturgy is the one place on earth where man is united, body and soul, with "the whole Christ" (CCC 795). For this reason, every Catholic must attend—and not just attend but *participate in*—the Mass on Sunday (the day of the week on which Jesus rose from the dead) and on holy days of obligation. Only those who receive the Eucharist worthily can have physical *and* spiritual unity with the resurrected Lord. In other words, because the human person is a body-spirit composite, a union of the whole person is made sacramentally possible only through reception of the consecrated bread and wine in the Holy Mass—this union of man with his Lord is aptly called Holy Communion. Protestants cannot deny that *if* the Eucharist is what the Catholic Church claims it is—Jesus *physically* present, though veiled behind the attributes of simple bread and wine—then there is nothing more essential to the Christian life than receiving it. There is no grace, no gift, more powerful than the person of Christ himself.

When I was young, I knew that we Catholics believed that Christ was physically present in the Blessed Sacrament; I don't remember doubting it. Yet I had difficulty marrying what I knew in my head to my heart. Overall, I was a pretty spiritual kid, praying every night before bed, memorizing Catholic prayers from the back of an old Children's Mass book, and being fascinated by stories of the saints and miracles (especially Marian apparitions). Nonetheless, I often found the Sunday Mass experience a bore. It was slow; the language was strange; the sermons were dry; the hymns were old; and for the most part I did not understand what was going on from one moment to the next. My parents and teachers tried to educate me about the parts of the Mass and their significance, but I just was not interested. I became more indifferent toward church and uninterested in spiritual things as I passed through my teenage years. My Sunday worship experience remained much the same as I entered young adulthood. Once I moved to the city for university, I attended some different Catholic parishes and even a more upbeat Baptist church, but it was all in vain. I was suffering from religious disenchantment.

I will never forget the first Mass I attended after my reconversion in my mid-twenties. It was in a little school chapel. I still had a child's understanding of the liturgy. I knew that the Bible readings were intended to keep the stories of the Old and New Testament fresh in our minds—especially the Gospels. They were also meant to inspire. I understood that the homily was meant to help us understand the Bible readings; that the profession of the Creed was intended to be a public confirmation of one's core beliefs; that the Eucharist—also known simply as "Communion"—united Christ's body with ours. But aside from these things, I understood the parts of the Mass and their deeper significance very little. Yet despite my ignorance, that very first Mass as a renewed Catholic was, for me, *breathtaking*. I found myself holding on to every word of the priest. I was attentive to the readings from the Old and New Testaments, and was captivated by the stories and messages they conveyed. And the Eucharist—ah, the Blessed Sacrament—*felt* like a true coming together of me and God. What I experienced that Sunday was a profound re-enchantment of the Mass.

Since my conversion, however, I have been to church hundreds of more times and, to be frank, the experience has often been dry—in the emotional sense, that is. And when you throw small children in the mix (we have two) the experience can be all the more . . . shall I say painful? Many people will relate to this. To take fidgety, noisy children to a slow, quiet Sunday Mass can be incredibly frustrating. Indeed, there are many things that can put a damper on our Mass experience, no matter how devout or theologically adept we might be. For many of us, our Monday-to-Saturday life is fast-paced and overscheduled. We are used to the continual stimulation of caffeine and conversation and screens. We are not used to the slowness and the silence of the liturgy. We are not used to the language of the Bible and the prayers. Even for us adults, it can be hard to slow down and settle into a day of rest—and especially into a solemn hour of prayer and worship. If only the Sunday Mass was more like Cirque du Soleil, right?

But the Eucharistic liturgy is the hinge of the Christian life; and we will not grasp the intrinsic value of the Mass until we understand that its aim is not to stimulate like entertainment: its aim is *to sanctify*. Although the Eucharist is the "source and summit of the Christian life (CCC 1324)," it is not uncommon for a Catholic—through no fault of his own—to feel almost nothing when he receives it. Since the grace received in the Eucharist is not a physical or emotional sensation but a *spiritual reality*, it tends to leave the emotions and senses unaffected. Hence, a Catholic's experience of Sunday Mass can leave him feeling that nothing special has gone on. This isn't because of a defect in the liturgy or the believer, but it calls the Catholic to a deeper faith in things not seen: "Blessed are those who have not seen and yet believe" (John 20:29).

The Mass presents an essential challenge to Catholics: in its slow and leisurely rhythm, in its moments of deep silence, in its demands of faith. Two grave dangers to the human soul are a lack of contemplation and lack of love. A human being cannot have enduring happiness without these two things. And the Mass fosters both because it, like nothing else, brings the ultimate object of contemplation and the very source of love—indeed, Love himself—to the faithful through the elevated hands of the priest. So the key to understanding why Catholics must attend Sunday Mass is above all in the essence of the Mass itself: Jesus Christ in the Eucharist. Our duty to be willing participants is not rooted in how it makes us feel but in what it is. As the sacred meeting place of God and man, the Mass reorients our lives toward God, reunites us with him in love, and thereby communicates the grace of salvation to our souls. In the long run, there can be nothing more productive—nothing more worth our time—than that.

The priesthood

In an interview with Oprah Winfrey, Evangelical pastor Carl Lentz of Hillsong Church in New York City explained why he believes Christianity has no place for priests:

> I believe our church is a conversation conduit where we're trying to teach people this is a conversation. You've got to sit at the table here. I can't sit there for you. *That's why Jesus came, so you didn't need a priest in the middle.* You don't need to go to a confessional booth. You can go straight to the source.[187]

My gut response was, "Where is *that* in the Bible?" I was provoked but not surprised, for this kind of waving aside of the priesthood is not uncommon. But anyone who *does* understand what the Catholic priesthood is will have no trouble seeing that Lentz, one of America's most influential pastors, is gravely misinformed. He seems to understand the priest to be an unnecessary middle man who interferes with one's personal relationship with God. But is this so? True, the Bible says that Christ is the *one* mediator between God and man (1 Tim. 2:5). And Paul's letter to the Hebrews asserts that Christ is the *one* high priest (Heb. 7:11–28). How then could a priesthood be necessary? It all comes down to distinctions. Let's look at this a little closer.

The false assumption that Lentz and many others make about the Catholic (and Eastern Orthodox) priesthood is that it interferes with Christ's one priesthood. They fail to consider another possibility: that the Catholic priesthood *participates* in Christ's priesthood. The *Catechism of the Catholic Church* explains:

> The redemptive sacrifice of Christ is unique, accomplished once for all; yet it is made present in the Eucharistic sacrifice of the Church. The same is true of the one priesthood of Christ; it is made present through the ministerial priesthood without diminishing the uniqueness of Christ's priesthood: "Only Christ is the true priest, the others being only his ministers" (1545).

When Christ suffered and died on the cross he offered himself, the Lamb of God, for the sins of the world. He was both priest and victim; and because he was God offering himself it was the perfect sacrifice. Now in heaven, Christ continues to offer himself before the throne of the Father: "And between the throne and the four living creatures and among the elders, I saw a Lamb standing, as though it had been slain" (Rev. 5:6). Jesus intercedes for us continually as the high priest and victim, until the whole world has been reconciled to him at the end of the age (Heb. 7:25). Scott Hahn explains:

> In other words, he who is our celebrant priest and reigning king in the liturgical worship of the heavenly assembly also appears continually as the Passover Lamb of the New Covenant. He appears as the Lamb because his sacrificial offering continues.[188]

Jesus is the unblemished Lamb of the New Covenant, the Lamb of God who takes away the sins of the world. This means that his sacrifice is the sacrifice to end all others. This is why Paul writes, "For even Christ our passover is sacrificed for us: Therefore let us keep the feast . . . with the unleavened bread of sincerity and truth" (1 Cor. 5:7, KJV). Indeed, Catholic priests everywhere continue to "keep the feast," fulfilling the words of the prophet Malachi that "from the rising of the sun to its setting my name is great among the nations, and in every place incense is offered to my name, and a pure offering."[189]

The Church has always understood the Mass, therefore, to be a remembrance of that once for all sacrifice of Christ, a participation in the New Covenant Passover sacrifice. The Mass is therefore essentially *sacrificial*. This is evident in the first century *Didache* which exhorts, "Assemble on the Lord's day, and break bread and offer the Eucharist; but first make confession of your faults, so that your sacrifice may be a pure one."[190] Now read the letter to the Hebrews. What word keeps popping up when the sacred author refers to Christ's high priesthood? *Melchizedek*. We are told that "Jesus has gone as a forerunner on our behalf, having become a high priest for ever after the order of Melchizedek" (Heb. 6:20). But who is Melchizedek? He is the mysterious priest-king who shows up in the book of Genesis, offering a sacrifice of bread and wine, and blessing Abram:

> And Melchizedek king of Salem brought out bread and wine; he was priest of God Most High. And he blessed [Abram] and said, "Blessed be Abram by God Most High, maker of heaven and earth" (Gen. 14:18–19).

This is an obvious foreshadowing of Jesus and his priests who offer a sacrifice of bread and wine in the New Covenant. Simple gifts of bread and wine are offered in every Mass—and in return God offers *himself,* as the bread and wine become his body and blood, under only the *appearance* of bread and wine. Jesus was the first to do this when he "took bread, and blessed, and broke it, and gave it to the disciples and said, "Take, eat; this is my body. Do this in remembrance of me" (Matt. 26:26; Luke 22:19).

St. John Vianney once remarked that if we truly knew the dignity of the priest, we would die, not out of fear, but out of love. How does this make sense? Well, it does so when we realize that priests can perform their duties only because of Christ working through them. That's why we say that the Catholic priest functions *in persona Christi*—*in the person of Christ*. St. Paul understood the priesthood's dependency on Christ's own presence and power when he taught, "Any one whom you forgive, I also forgive. What I have forgiven, if I have forgiven anything, has been for your sake *in the presence of Christ*" (2 Cor. 2:10). Here Paul is referring to the "ministry of reconciliation" conferred by Jesus onto the apostles, through which they obtained the authority to forgive sins "in his presence" (2 Cor. 5:18). Indeed, to be ordained a priest through "the laying on of hands" is to receive the most precious of gifts. This is why Paul writes to Timothy, "I remind you to rekindle *the gift of God* that is within you through the laying on of my hands" (2 Tim. 1:6), and again to the young priest in another letter:

> Till I come, attend to the public reading of scripture, to preaching, to teaching. Do not neglect *the gift* you have, which was given you by prophetic utterance when the elders laid their hands upon you (1 Tim. 4:13–14).

Perhaps the most obvious problem with Lentz's objection is the explicit and overwhelming presence of the priesthood in the early Church, from the first century onward. In the Acts of the Apostles we are told the first Christians "devoted themselves to the apostles' teaching and fellowship, to the breaking of bread and the prayers" (Acts 2:42). Later we are told, "On the first day of the week, [they] were gathered together to break bread" (Acts 20:7).

Recall how Ignatius of Antioch, a disciple of St. John, referred to the hierarchy of bishop, priest, and deacon in his letter to the Magnesians (c. A.D. 110). And consider the words of St. Clement of Alexandria, written around 208. He leaves no room for doubt that the priests of the early Church, along with the bishops and deacons, were not to be seen as hindrances to a life of holiness, but as symbols of the heavenly holiness that is promised to all who believe and walk in grace and obedience:

Even here in the Church the gradations of bishops, presbyters, and deacons happen to be imitations, in my opinion, of the angelic glory and of that arrangement which, the scriptures say, awaits those who have followed in the footsteps of the apostles and who have lived in complete righteousness according to the gospel.[191]

Making sense of the Eucharist

We are what we eat. When we dine at our own tables, the food we take in is eventually broken down and united to our body. But something infinitely different happens in the sacrament of the Eucharist. When a Catholic goes to Mass and participates in Holy Communion, his food does not become him; rather, he becomes like his food. He becomes like Jesus Christ himself; and this surpasses all other forms of worship, because only in the Mass can a Christian be united with Christ spiritually and bodily.

The Eucharist—the Blessed Sacrament—is the central "thing" of the Catholic life: because it is God. Catholics believe that during the Mass, which is a reenactment of the Last Supper, when the priest holds up the unleavened bread as Christ did and says the words of Christ—"This is my body"—the bread actually changes from bread to God, while maintaining the appearance of bread. The physical properties stay the same; but it changes in substance.

Several years ago my sister, Larissa, and I stood in our parents' kitchen, debating the real presence of Jesus in the Eucharist. By that time I had drifted away from the Church; she was a campus missionary. My faith in Catholic teachings had long since turned to skepticism—and the "real presence" was at the top of the list. To me it seemed obvious that the bread remained bread, and the wine remained wine; there was clearly no physical change to either.

Larissa listened patiently to me, and as we closed our kitchen debate she made an intriguing suggestion: that I investigate the "Miracle of Lanciano." What I discovered was the impetus to the first of my many steps back to the Church of Rome.

In the eighth century, a monk who had doubts about the real presence of Christ in the Eucharist was offering Mass in the Italian town of Lanciano. During the Mass, when he pronounced the words of consecration, the host was miraculously changed into actual human cardiac tissue and the wine became real human blood. The blood later coagulated, while the flesh remained as it was. Neither has decomposed. In more recent times, scientific investigations have been carried out which have all reached the same conclusion: there is no natural explanation for why the flesh and blood are resisting decomposition. In Lanciano today you can still see the miraculous flesh and blood from that eighth-century Mass.

Many such Eucharistic miracles have occurred through the centuries. They are one way Christ has helped the faithful to believe in this "hard teaching." Most Catholics, however, neither require nor have the opportunity to see such a miracle. The body of Christ, hidden behind the "veil" of bread, has a convincing power all its own. As J.R.R. Tolkien once wrote to his son, "Out of the darkness of my life, so much frustrated, I put before you the one great thing to love on earth: the Blessed Sacrament. . . . There you will find romance, glory, honor, fidelity, and the true way of all your loves on earth."[192]

The Eucharist is not to be merely adored from a distance like the burning bush; it is meant to be approached—and *consumed*. John's Gospel reveals clearly that Jesus commanded a *literal* eating and drinking of his body and blood (John 6:32–71). That Jesus meant this in exactly this way can be drawn from a few hints in the Gospels.

First, consider the disciples' reactions to Jesus' words "my flesh is true food and my blood is true drink" (John 6:55). Many left him when he said it. This is the only instance in the Gospels that Jesus lost followers because of *doctrine*. Also consider Jesus' choice of wording. In the Greek translation, Jesus begins with the verb that translates "to eat" (as in "eat my flesh") and when his followers are scandalized by his teaching, he resorts to even stronger language, using the word for "gnaw." He is clearly emphasizing the *literal* sense of His teaching, making no attempt to soften it or give it a more tolerable *symbolic* meaning. His teaching on the Eucharist was a hard one and he knew it; and if any doubt or ambiguity remained, he made his meaning unmistakable at the Last Supper when he said, "Take, eat; this is my body" (Matt. 26:26). In recording this event, Paul reinforces the grave importance of receiving the sacrament worthily when he warns, "Whoever, therefore, eats the bread or drinks the cup of the Lord in an unworthy manner will be guilty of profaning the body and blood of the Lord" (1 Cor. 11:23–29).

A disciple of John, Ignatius of Antioch, wrote at the beginning of the second century, "I have no taste for corruptible food nor for the pleasures of this life. I desire the bread of God, which is the flesh of Jesus Christ, who was of the seed of David; and for drink I desire his blood, which is love incorruptible." In another letter Ignatius declared, "The Eucharist is the flesh of our savior Jesus Christ, flesh which suffered for our sins and which that Father, in his goodness, raised up again. They who deny the gift of God are perishing in their disputes."

The Eucharist requires faith. We have good reason to believe Christ is really present in it, but no scientific experiment or philosophical argument can prove it. It is a pure gift to those who have faith, and folly to everyone else. But believers are not to avoid the Eucharist out of a lack of understanding or out of a lack of holiness. It is, after all, medicine for the sinful and food for the spirit.

The sacrament of the Eucharist is for every Christian because it is the only way to enter into *total* communion with God in this life. And because the Eucharist is Christ's body, and the Church is Christ's body, to be united with Christ in the Eucharist is to be united with all the other people of God on earth and in heaven. It is the defining sacrament of Christian unity because it *is* Christ, and only in him do all things hold together. That is why it is the source and summit of the Christian life (CCC 1324). Nothing else compares.

12

Unity as Church

Toronto is a long way from home, being in Eastern Canada. I'm from the Wild West (Saskatchewan precisely) and, for that reason, while studying chiropractic in Toronto I didn't always get home on holidays. One year, a classmate invited me to spend Thanksgiving weekend on his family farm. He was an evangelical Christian, and he knew I was a practicing Catholic. On our drive out to the farm he warned me, "My dad is a pretty bold guy. When he finds out you're Catholic, he's probably going to ask you a few questions—just to warn you." I wasn't sure whether to be excited or worried. Was this going to be a *long* "long weekend?" Sure enough, the following evening the three of us were relaxing in the living room when, as promised, my buddy's father leaned forward in his chair and asked, "So Matt. Are you having a good weekend?" I was having a great time, I replied. "Good—and you're Catholic I hear." I said yes, feeling confident (so far my answers were spot on!). He then went on to rave about a Catholic priest who had recently been brought into their evangelical church for a question-and-answer period. "Very helpful," he recalled. "But I still have some questions. One in particular is in regard to your praying to saints. Why not just go straight to God?" Classic, I thought. "Mr. Smith, can I ask you a question? If you were really sick and needed all the prayers you could get, would you hesitate to ask the people in your life that are closest to God—say, your pastor—to pray for you?" "Of course not," he replied. Then I asked him, "But why not go straight to God?" After a moment of reflection, he said, "That's a *great* point, Matt. I've never thought about it that way before. I'm going to have to give that some more thought." That was the last religious conversation we had that weekend, but I had planted a seed in his mind (perhaps more of a pebble in his shoe). That is what evangelization is all about: planting seeds. "I planted, Apollos watered," writes St. Paul, "but God gave the growth" (1 Cor. 3:6–8).

The communion of saints

My friend's dad showed that he was honest and reasonable. He was committed but not obstinate in his Protestant convictions; his resulting openness to my response allowed new light to be shed on what he found a difficult-to-accept Catholic teaching. This is not easy for everybody. In my experience, praying to the saints is one of the most scandalous Catholic practices for Protestants. They see it as akin to divination or some other occult practice, failing to see the difference between conjuring evil spirits for one's private purposes, and asking a brother or sister in Christ for help in furthering the will of God. They fail to see that those who are in heaven are in a sense *more* alive and capable of greater things than we are—because they are perfectly in Christ. Jesus reminds his disciples that God in the Old Testament said he is "the God of Abraham, and the God of Isaac, and the God of Jacob"; but then our Lord asserts that God "is not God of the dead, but of the living" (Matt. 22:32). Abraham, Isaac, and Jacob were dead physically, yes, but not spiritually. Similarly, at the Transfiguration, don't we find Jesus conversing with Moses? Likewise, when Catholics pray to the saints, they pray not to the dead but to the living.

There are not two Churches, one on earth and one in heaven. *There is one Church, at once earthly and heavenly.* This is the key to understanding the doctrine of the Communion of Saints which, when properly understood, makes sense of the practice of praying to the saints. The communion of saints is professed in the ancient Apostles' Creed and elsewhere. But what is it? The *Catechism of the Catholic Church* puts it in the simplest of terms: "The communion of saints is the Church"; it then adds:

> All of us, however, in varying degrees and in different ways share in the same charity towards God and our neighbors, and

we all sing the one hymn of glory to our God. All, indeed, who are of Christ and who have his Spirit form one Church and in Christ cleave together (946).

Trying to understand how lowly sinners on earth can be united with the "spirits of just men made perfect" (Heb. 12:23) in heaven can be difficult, especially in light of the scandals and hypocrisy that have rocked the Church at different times in history, including now. But if we sinners can enjoy union with Christ in this life through faith—and this is precisely what Christ made possible—it follows that we can enjoy communion with the rest of heaven in this life: because all of heaven is in Christ. St. Paul, though a great saint, was also a sinner. He was keenly aware of his own brokenness—a mark of the greatest saints. As Peter Kreeft writes, "There are only two kinds of people: sinners, who think they're saints; and saints, who know they're sinners."[193] That is truly a profound thing to contemplate. Paul candidly laments, "For I know that nothing good dwells within me, that is, in my flesh. I can will what is right, but I cannot do it. For I do not do the good I want, but the evil I do not want is what I do" (Rom. 7:18–19). Yet at the same time he can write, "I have been crucified with Christ; it is no longer I who live, but Christ who lives in me," and "we, though many, are one body in Christ, and individually members one of another" (Gal. 2:20, Rom. 12:5). Paul makes it clear that although we are damaged by sin, it is possible for Christians to be united with *and in* Christ by grace.

We have already seen how the sacrament of the Holy Eucharist, above all, makes it possible for Christians to have a mystical union with Christ, while equally effecting a union of all members of the Church. It is the life-giving love of Christ, not our biological life, that effects the deepest unity within the Church. Scripture tells us that it is good to pray for one another. Why should we think that death would make it impossible for those in heaven to continue praying, out of love, for those still fighting the good fight on earth? Paul preaches that death has no power to destroy our union in Christ:

For I am sure that neither death, nor life, nor angels, nor prin-
cipalities, nor things present, nor things to come, nor powers,
nor height, nor depth, nor anything else in all creation, will
be able to separate us from the love of God in Christ Jesus our
Lord (Rom. 8:38–39).

The "one mediator" argument

You cannot have communion without communication. The greater your communication is with another person, the greater your
communion will be. That is why a mother experiences such a profound attachment to her child, whom she was once united with
in the flesh. They share the same "blood" as it were, cut from the
same genetic cloth. There is much between a mother and child
that is shared, before birth and afterward. Perhaps the only earthly
communion that is deeper than that is what exists between husband
and wife. When a sacramental union is formed between man and
woman it is unbreakable; only death can sunder it. In the mari-
tal covenant there is a singular communion of flesh, mind, will,
experience, and property. As John Paul the Great taught us in his
theology of the body, there is no union that better signifies the perfect communion of persons in the Blessed Trinity than marriage.
Nuptial communion is the most fitting symbol of the love of God.

But heaven offers us something greater. That is why Jesus
tells us in the Gospel of Matthew that in the resurrection we
will neither marry nor be given in marriage (Matt. 22:30). The
union of persons we will experience after the resurrection of the
body will be indescribably superior to the sexual union or any
other kind of human intimacy that exists in this life. This is hard
for us to grasp and impossible to imagine; but so is a thousand-
sided polygon. That we cannot possibly imagine how this could
be so, does not mean it is false. It is not. We have the Lord's
word. The point is this: how the communion of persons works
in the kingdom of God is largely a mystery. Christians should
not shun the concept of praying to saints and angels just because
it is difficult to understand how they would receive them.

Do they "hear" our prayers? We don't know—but it's not as if God couldn't arrange that if he wanted to. And how does, say, the Blessed Virgin Mary hear thousands of individual prayers at once during a public rosary at the Vatican? We don't know, but we do know that time does not operate in heaven as it does here. What we *do* know is that the saints and angels in heaven receive our prayers and offer them on our behalf to God.

The Bible says so. In the Book of Revelation, John gives an account of "elders" in heaven offering the prayers of the saints before Jesus, the Lamb:

> And between the throne and the four living creatures and among the elders, I saw a lamb standing, as though it had been slain. . . . And when he had taken the scroll, the four living creatures and the twenty-four elders fell down before the lamb, each holding a harp, and with golden bowls full of incense, which are the prayers of the saints (Rev 5:8).

Three chapters later John recalls a vision of angels before the throne of God, offering the prayers of the saints with incense:

> And another angel came and stood at the altar with a golden censer; and he was given much incense to mingle with the prayers of all the saints upon the golden altar before the throne; and the smoke of the incense rose with the prayers of the saints from the hand of the angel before God (Rev. 8:3–4).

"But hold on!" our separated brethren might object. When a person prays to a saint, isn't he attributing to mere creatures what should only be attributed to the Creator—the ability to intercede for others before God. Doesn't the Bible say in Revelation (8:3–4) that "there is one God; there is also one mediator between God and humankind, Christ Jesus"? (2 Tim. 2:1–5).

How should a Catholic respond to this? First, we must remember that when interpreting passages of Scripture, the passage should be interpreted in light of the *whole* Bible. Second, "to pray" does not necessarily mean "to worship." It can also mean to request or plead. Have you ever heard the outdated English phrase "pray tell me," as in "Pray tell me, have you seen Harry this morning?" In this context the word indicates a plea or request. This is the same context Catholics assume when praying to the saints and angels. Prayer to God, on the other hand, is an act of worship due to God alone. Praying to saints is qualitatively different. The moral is that Catholics should pray "straight to God" and "through the angels to God." It is not a matter of either/or but rather of both/and, since communion with the saints is just an *indirect*—but still wholly efficacious—way of uniting ourselves to "the whole Christ," that is, the Church.

Third, by requesting the intercession of the saints we make our prayers more powerful. James tells us that "the prayer of a righteous man has great power in its effects" (James 5:16). And since the saints in heaven have been made perfect in righteousness, their prayers are all the more powerful. Even the greatest saint on earth would benefit from the prayers of the "spirits of just men made perfect."

Fourth, Jesus welcomes us to participate in his singular mediatorship. If that were not the case, how else could we make sense of this verse from Paul's letter to the Colossians?

> Now I rejoice in my sufferings for your sake, and in my flesh I complete what is lacking in Christ's afflictions for the sake of his body, that is, the church (Col. 1:24).

Is Paul mistaken? Was there something lacking in Christ's sufferings? Yes and no. On the one hand, Christ's sacrifice is complete. As the true mediator between God and man—as the God-Man—Jesus' offering of his own life was infinitely meritorious. The redemption of the world has been irreversibly put into effect. But on the other hand, as mystically united members of Christ's body, we can unite our sufferings to his—and make *our* sufferings redemptive.

It is worth going back to the passage that sparked this discussion. Look what Paul writes only a few verses before the "one mediator" verse:

First of all, then, *I urge that supplications, prayers, intercessions, and thanksgivings be made for everyone,* kings and all who are in high positions, so that we may lead a quiet and peaceable life in all godliness and dignity. This is right and is acceptable in the sight of God our Savior, who desires everyone to be saved and to come to the knowledge of the truth (1 Tim. 2:1).

Here, St. Paul urges that we mediate for one another through prayer. This is not necessary in the strictest sense because God knows all our needs and wants, and he knows what our prayers will be before we do. But just as we participate in co-creating new human beings and converting nonbelievers (God could do these things without us), he allows for us to enter into the lives of others, providing opportunities for us to love, and *grow* in love, for others.

So, with the "one mediator" argument sufficiently addressed, and a reasonable case put forth for prayers to the souls made righteous in heaven, we should be able to rest easy. We have good reason to join ourselves to the "great cloud of witnesses" (Heb. 12:1) in prayer, charity, and faith. For we have in those witnesses, not just intercessors, but friends whom we hope to know intimately, face-to-face, one day. Until then, let us never cease to join King David in his prayer of praise launched to the heavens:

Bless the Lord, O you his angels, you mighty ones who do his bidding, obedient to his spoken word. . . . Praise him, all his angels; praise him, all his host! (Ps. 103:20; 148:2).

Christ's mother and ours

The biblical view of Mary is that she has been specially set apart by God in the order of grace. Elizabeth, filled with the Holy Spirit, was one of the first to affirm this when she proclaimed Mary's blessedness upon her visitation to Elizabeth's home:

And when Elizabeth heard the greeting of Mary, the babe leaped in her womb; and Elizabeth was filled with the Holy Spirit and she exclaimed with a loud cry, "Blessed are you among women, and blessed is the fruit of your womb!" (Luke 1:41–42).

If St. James is right—if the prayer of the righteous is great in its effects—then a prayerful relationship with Mary is indispensable for the Christian, for she is the greatest of the saints. One reason the Virgin Mary is set apart is the depth of her "yes" to God's plan—and because of God's "yes" to her. Following her consent to bear the Christ child, her flesh was united with the body of Christ in the most literal sense. No other woman will ever experience this kind of union with Christ, this mother-child *communion*. By this fact alone, Mary is blessed among women, and all of humanity for that matter.

Now to steal a phrase from Einstein: God does not play dice. So Mary was not *randomly* endowed with her maternal role. Rather, from all eternity, she was *chosen* by God for the task. She was favored by God to bear him, to raise him, to laugh with him—to suffer with him. The point here can be deceivingly simple: if God has honored Mary so singularly, shouldn't we? If we are to reverence the mothers of our friends and relatives, shouldn't we *a fortiori* reverence the mother of our Lord? Any Christian who fails to honor Mary, if not in their words then at least in their heart, has a disordered relationship with the mother of Christ.

And Mary is also *our* spiritual mother, because of her cooperative role in bringing into this world the Savior who would make it possible for man to be "born again." The Fathers of the Second Vatican Council put it this way:

> In a wholly singular way she cooperated by her obedience, faith, hope, and burning charity in the Savior's work of restoring supernatural life to souls. For this reason she is a mother to us in the order of grace (*Lumen Gentium* 61).

This spiritual motherhood is hinted at in John's Gospel when Jesus speaks the words, "Woman, behold your son" to Mary, who stands at the foot of the cross with John, and then says "Behold your mother" to the beloved apostle (John 19:26–27). And though our Lord speaks these words in a literal sense to Mary and John (conferring upon them a kind of "step" relationship), he speaks them in a spiritual sense to the Church throughout the ages. Thus, St. Augustine would write:

> That one woman is both mother and virgin, not in spirit only but even in body. In spirit she is mother, not of our head, who is our Savior himself—of whom all, even she herself, are rightly called children of the bridegroom—*but plainly she is the mother of us* who are his members.[194]

The Church holds to the sacred tradition that, from the moment of her existence, Mary was endowed by God with perfect sanctity. In 1854 Pope Pius IX declared in the papal bull *Ineffabilis Deus*:

> We declare, pronounce and define that the doctrine which asserts that the Blessed Virgin Mary, from the first moment of her conception, by a singular grace and privilege of almighty God, and in view of the merits of Jesus Christ, Saviour of the human race, was preserved free from every stain of original sin is a doctrine revealed by God.

Pius's dogmatic declaration was not a nineteenth-century invention pulled out of thin air. Its purpose was to affirm once and for all, as all *ex cathedra* statements do, a tradition passed down since the age of the apostles. Although Paul wrote that "all have sinned" (Rom. 3:23), the context is personal sin—that is, sin which is *done* rather than inherited (Paul deals with original sin two chapters later). So, have *all* sinned? In general, yes. But there are exceptions—including Jesus himself. Others include infants and the severely mentally handicapped, since a sufficient degree of knowledge and consent are required to sin culpably.

And although Eve, like Mary, was conceived without sin, unlike Eve, Mary did not fall. That is why John Henry Newman, drawing from the writings of the early Church Fathers, fittingly called Mary "the daughter of Eve unfallen." Indeed, the earliest Church Fathers hinted at Mary's sinlessness in their writings when they referred or alluded to Mary as the second or *new* Eve. Irenaeus, for example, writes in the second century that "the knot of Eve's disobedience was loosed by the obedience of Mary. What the virgin Eve had bound in unbelief, the Virgin Mary loosed through faith."[195] The later Church Fathers conveyed the blessedness of Mary even more explicitly. Consider the words of St. Ephraim:

> You alone and your Mother are more beautiful than any others, for there is no blemish in you nor any stains upon your Mother. Who of my children can compare in beauty to these?[196]

Mary's Immaculate Conception was not explicitly defined (so far as we know given the ancient writings we have) by the earliest Church Fathers. But if such a belief was incongruent with the earliest Christian tradition, we might have expected a sort of hostility to such a suggestion when the doctrine finally bubbled to the surface. But we have no evidence that the doctrine was ever challenged as a heresy by the early Church. As time moved forward, deep reverence for Mary, immaculately conceived, was sustained. Even Martin Luther believed it, professing in a 1527 sermon:

> It is a sweet and pious belief that the infusion of Mary's soul was effected without original sin; so that in the very infusion of her soul she was also purified from original sin and adorned with God's gifts, receiving a pure soul.[197]

Finally, it is mportant to consider how the angel Gabriel greets Mary in John's Gospel: "Hail, full of grace" (Luke 1:28). No one else in the Bible receives an angelic greeting in this way—by a *title*. Just as we might show respect to a physician by calling him "Doctor," or a judge "Honorable," Mary was called "Full of Grace" by this messenger from heaven—and an angel never speaks anything but *exactly* what God wants him to speak. This explains why Mary, in all her humility, "was greatly troubled at the saying, and considered in her mind what sort of greeting this might be" (Luke 1:29). Thus, if an archangel of God greets her with such reverence—and if the likes of Irenaeus, Newman, and Luther write and speak about her with such respect—should not we also?

As St. Ambrose observed, Mary's life was "like a mirror reflecting the face of chastity and the form of virtue."[198] We have ample reason to believe that Mary was an exemplar of obedience and humility—a perfect model of holiness—and as such we can do no better than to recruit her as our maternal intercessor. No one understands our dependence on God's grace greater than she, Christ's mother and ours, whose sweet voice proclaimed in the home of Elizabeth:

My soul magnifies the Lord,
and my spirit rejoices in God my Savior,
for he has regarded the low estate of his handmaiden.
For behold, henceforth all generations will call me blessed
(Luke 1:47–48).

Evangelizing the Indifferent

"Do not be afraid. Open wide the doors for Christ!"

—St. John Paul the Great

Shortly before World War II, Archbishop Fulton Sheen famously observed that "there are not one hundred people in the United States who hate the Catholic Church, but there are millions who hate what they wrongly believe to be the Catholic Church."[199] What the venerable archbishop had identified was the problem of mass ignorance about Catholicism. The problem remains, and it is not limited to the United States. It likely will not go away until the deeper issue of religious indifference is addressed, and hearts and minds are awakened.

The number of dereligionized people in North America and Europe is rapidly rising. In particular, the number of people who consider themselves *unaffiliated* with any religion—also known as the "Nones"—has surged remarkably. According to the most recent surveys, the number of Nones in the United States has risen from about fifteen percent to approximately one quarter of the population—just over the past decade.[200] No doubt there are analogous trends in Canada and the rest of the Western world. So we are faced with a problem—and one that seems to be getting worse. What then can be done?

An action plan

I propose two overall solutions to the problem of religious indifference, one immediate and the other precautionary. First, we must immediately engage the indifferentists and awaken them from their intellectual slumber. Second, we must teach our children how to think clearly and critically about their faith. This book will be helpful primarily in equipping Catholics to implement the first solution. But it may also serve as an aid to the second.

For a more concrete plan of action for evangelizing the indifferent we might follow Pascal's program outlined in the *Pensées*:

> *Order.* Men despise religion. They hate it and are afraid it may be true. The cure for this is first [1] to show that religion is not contrary to reason, but worthy of reverence and respect. Next [2] make it attractive, make good men wish it were true, and then [3] show that it is.[201]

Three different steps for evangelizing the indifferent are suggested here. Depending on circumstances, the steps may be taken in a different order. Bishop Robert Barron, one of the great evangelists of our time, has advocated that we begin with *beauty*, what he has called "the arrowhead of evangelization" (step 2). Here, however, I will consider them in the order laid out by Pascal. How you implement them and in what order will depend ultimately on you, and the person you are evangelizing.

First, we establish a first principle in apologetics: that there is compatibility between faith and reason. Atheists often like to define faith as "holding a belief in the absence of any evidence" or "believing something despite stronger evidence for the contrary." But these definitions are loaded dice. So here's rule number one: *don't let skeptics define your terms for you.* Properly understood, faith is assent to a proposition based on the authority of another. Faith is never opposed to evidence; but it is open to more than just, say, scientific evidence. John Paul the Great famously asserted that "faith and reason are like two wings on which the human spirit rises to the contemplation of truth."[202] It is the duty of every Christian to defend this compatibility by knowing what he believes and why. We can do this by defining key terms like *faith* and *mystery*. We can also do this by showing that our beliefs are not blindly held on to despite contrary evidence, but are based on solid philosophical, historical, theological, and scientific grounds.

Second, make Christianity attractive: make indifferentists desire it to be true. In his 1970 Nobel Lecture in Literature, Alexandr Solzhenitsyn, the Russian novelist and survivor of the Soviet gulags, asserted that "the convincingness of a true work of art is completely irrefutable and it forces even an opposing heart to surrender."[203] Writers like Lewis and Tolkien, poets like Dante and Hopkins, musicians like Palestrina and Bach, artists like Michelangelo and Giotto, have proven this true. Each, in his own creative way, has brought countless people to their knees through the enchanting power of beauty. Each, in his own way, has functioned as a kind of baptizer of the imagination. The evidential power of beauty is something that is especially significant to our current project, because in an age where truth and goodness are trivialized by indifferentism and moral relativism, the imagination remains an open portal of entry for evangelization. Beauty is, I think, the most potent remedy against modernity's imaginative sterility and "contracted common sense" Chesterton spoke so critically of.

Simply preaching the good news of Jesus Christ has been effective in every age of Church history. We must also tell the story of salvation and tell it well, beginning with the Old Testament as the earliest Christians did. Salvation history is a great adventure, and if we tell it well we may draw others into it.

Third, we show that Christianity *is* true. "Always be prepared to make a defense to anyone who calls you to account for the hope that is in you," exhorts St. Peter (1 Pet. 5). We are all called to make a case for the Faith, in word and in action. Our lives should serve as visible evidence that we know the good news and live joyfully because of it. Our lives—like the architecture, arts, and letters of Christian artists—should be a sort of aesthetic apologetic, a visible display of goodness and beauty. We must also appeal to the intellect of indifferentists by means of questioning, dialogue, and argumentation.

Pascal's approach, of course, runs on the assumption that your first action as a missionary to the indifferentists is *prayer*. This, and indeed any evangelistic effort, will almost surely be fruitless if you fail to invite the Holy Spirit into your missionary work. For the conversion of the other, but also for our own perseverance in apostolic labor, we must pray above all. "Only the interior life can sustain us in the hidden, backbreaking labor of planting the seed that seems to go so long without fruit," writes Dom Chautard.[204] More important, we too must be in the continual state of conversion—praying, reading Scripture, meditating on the truths of the Faith, and seeking a living relationship with our one Lord and Savior, Jesus Christ. Open wide the doors for Christ—do that first—for your own sake. That "first step" is the secret to successfully opening the doors wide to Christ for others. To most effectively take Jesus Christ to others, we need to *know* our Lord and we need to *be like* him. Consider Bishop Barron's words:

> What solves the [modern] problem, what indicates a way forward, is not an abstraction or a new philosophical conception but this Jesus, this incarnate Lord, crucified and risen from the dead. It is this Christ who rubs healing salve into sin-sick eyes; it is this Christ who, reflected iconically in his saints, provides the template for right living.[205]

This approach to engaging the indifferent is fundamental. But, as in other things, the fundamentals are often what is most needed. Truth, goodness, beauty: all three of these "transcendentals" have a peculiar way of defending themselves. You do not need to have *all* the answers yourself (what apologist does?) to awaken the indifferent. You have likely heard this before, but it is worth repeating: *what is often more important than having the right answers is asking the right questions.*

Can indifference ever be justified? Well, sure, when it comes to the unimportant things. But people are often mistaken about what is important, and I wonder if most cases of religious indifference are more the result of ignorance than arrogance. People don't *know* that God is the ground of their existence and all moral truth. They don't *know* that Jesus Christ is their Savior and the secret to everlasting fulfillment. They don't *know* that the Catholic Church is founded by Christ himself upon the apostles and their successors. People don't know these things, not because they have not been told, but because they have not been shown. Let's show them.

I have already outlined three distinct types of religious indifference—closed, open, and denominational—each of which reflects a different degree of indifference, and each therefore demanding its own approach. Often the easiest and most effective launching point for an apologist is asking a question. Your starting point should be a strategy for determining the indifferentist's starting point. Start with a general question to set things up. Then sit back. For the closed indifferentist, you might start with, *Why (or why not) should a person worship God?* For the open indifferentist, *Why (or why not) worship Jesus?* For the denominational indifferentist, *Why (or why not) worship in the Catholic Church?* Ask whichever question is most direct to the type of indifferentism you are facing, and you're off to the races!

Finally, after identifying which doctrines of Catholicism your interlocutor rejects or is indifferent to, you will want to help him to understand the cost of rejecting those beliefs. By turning his back on God, he rejects the very ground of his own existence and of objective morality. By rejecting Jesus Christ he rejects his divine Lord and Savior. And by rejecting the Catholic Church in its doctrine and sacraments he rejects full communion with the Church founded upon Christ—and even Christ himself. There are no doctrines of the Catholic Church that are entirely inconsequential for the thriving of the human person. Orthodoxy is the surest path to salvation. Hold to the doctrine, says St. Paul, because by doing so you will save yourself—and others (1 Tim. 4:16). Doctrine matters because truth matters; and truth matters because it keeps us living in the real world, the only world in which is found the ascending path to everlasting fulfillment.

Blaise Pascal on Indifference

Blaise Pascal on Indifference[206]

Let them at least learn what is the religion they attack, before attacking it. If this religion boasted of having a clear view of God, and of possessing it open and unveiled, it would be attacking it to say that we see nothing in the world which shows it with this clearness. But since, on the contrary, it says that men are in darkness and estranged from God, that he has hidden himself from their knowledge, that this is in fact the name which he gives himself in the scriptures, *Deus absconditus*; and finally, if it endeavours equally to establish these two things: that God has set up in the Church visible signs to make himself known to those who should seek him sincerely, and that he has nevertheless so disguised them that he will only be perceived by those who seek him with all their heart; what advantage can they obtain, when, in the negligence with which they make profession of being in search of the truth, they cry out that nothing reveals it to them; and since that darkness in which they are, and with which they upbraid the Church, establishes only one of the things which she affirms, without touching the other, and, very far from destroying, proves her doctrine?

In order to attack it, they should have protested that they had made every effort to seek him everywhere, and even in that which the Church proposes for their instruction, but without satisfaction. If they talked in this manner, they would in truth be attacking one of her pretensions. But I hope here to show that no reasonable person can speak thus, and I venture even to say that no one has ever done so. We know well enough how those who are of this mind behave. They believe they have made great efforts for their instruction when they have spent a few hours in reading some book of Scripture and have questioned some priests on the truths of the faith. After that, they boast of having made vain search in books and among men. But, verily, I will tell them what I have often said, that this negligence is insufferable.

We are not here concerned with the trifling interests of some stranger, that we should treat it in this fashion; the matter concerns ourselves and our all. The immortality of the soul is a matter which is of so great consequence to us and which touches us so profoundly that we must have lost all feeling to be indifferent as to knowing what it is. All our actions and thoughts must take such different courses, according as there are or are not eternal joys to hope for, that it is impossible to take one step with sense and judgment unless we regulate our course by our view of this point which ought to be our ultimate end. Thus our first interest and our first duty is to enlighten ourselves on this subject, whereon depends all our conduct.

Therefore among those who do not believe, I make a vast difference between those who strive with all their power to inform themselves and those who live without troubling or thinking about it. I can have only compassion for those who sincerely bewail their doubt, who regard it as the greatest of misfortunes, and who, sparing no effort to escape it, make of this inquiry their principal and most serious occupation. But as for those who pass their life without thinking of this ultimate end of life, and who, for this sole reason that they do not find within themselves the lights which convince them of it, neglect to seek them elsewhere, and to examine thoroughly whether this opinion is one of those which people receive with credulous simplicity, or one of those which, although obscure in themselves, have nevertheless a solid and immovable foundation, I look upon them in a manner quite different.

This carelessness in a matter which concerns themselves, their eternity, their all, moves me more to anger than pity; it astonishes and shocks me; it is to me monstrous. I do not say this out of the pious zeal of a spiritual devotion. I expect, on the contrary, that we ought to have this feeling from principles of human interest and self-love; for this we need only see what the least enlightened persons see. We do not require great education of the mind to understand that here is no real and lasting satisfaction; that our pleasures are only vanity; that our evils are infinite; and, lastly, that death, which threatens us every moment, must infallibly place us within a few years under the dreadful necessity of being for ever either annihilated or unhappy.

There is nothing more real than this, nothing more terrible. Be we as heroic as we like, that is the end which awaits the world. Let us reflect on this and then say whether it is not beyond doubt that there is no good in this life but in the hope of another; that we are happy only in proportion as we draw near it; and that, as there are no more woes for those who have complete assurance of eternity, so there is no more happiness for those who have no insight into it.

Surely then it is a great evil thus to be in doubt, but it is at least an indispensable duty to seek when we are in such doubt; and thus the doubter who does not seek is altogether completely unhappy and completely wrong. And if besides this he is easy and content, professes to be so, and indeed boasts of it; if it is this state itself which is the subject of his joy and vanity, I have no words to describe so silly a creature. How can people hold these opinions? What joy can we find in the expectation of nothing but hopeless misery? What reason for boasting that we are in impenetrable darkness?

And how can it happen that the following argument occurs to a reasonable man?

"I know not who put me into the world, nor what the world is, nor what I myself am. I am in terrible ignorance of everything. I know not what my body is, nor my senses, nor my soul, not even that part of me which thinks what I say, which reflects on all and on itself, and knows itself no more than the rest. I see those frightful spaces of the universe which surround me, and I find myself tied to one corner of this vast expanse, without knowing why I am put in this place rather than in another, nor why the short time which is given me to live is assigned to me at this point rather than at another of the whole eternity which was before me or which shall come after me. I see nothing but infinites on all sides, which surround me as an atom and as a shadow which endures only for an instant and returns no more. All I know is that I must soon die, but what I know least is this very death which I cannot escape.

"As I know not whence I come, so I know not whither I go. I know only that, in leaving this world, I fall for ever either into annihilation or into the hands of an angry God, without knowing to which of these two states I shall be for ever assigned. Such is my state, full of weakness and uncertainty. And from all this I conclude that I ought to spend all the days of my life without caring to inquire into what must happen to me. Perhaps I might find some solution to my doubts, but I will not take the trouble, nor take a step to seek it; and after treating with scorn those who are concerned with this care, I will go without foresight and without fear to try the great event, and let myself be led carelessly to death, uncertain of the eternity of my future state."

Who would desire to have for a friend a man who talks in this fashion? Who would choose him out from others to tell him of his affairs? Who would have recourse to him in affliction? And indeed to what use in life could one put him? In truth, it is the glory of religion to have for enemies men so unreasonable; and their opposition to it is so little dangerous that it serves, on the contrary, to establish its truths. For the Christian faith goes mainly to establish these two facts: the corruption of nature, and redemption by Jesus Christ.

Now I contend that, if these men do not serve to prove the truth of the redemption by the holiness of their behaviour, they at least serve admirably to show the corruption of nature by sentiments so unnatural. Nothing is so important to man as his own state, nothing is so formidable to him as eternity; and thus it is not natural that there should be men indifferent to the loss of their existence, and to the perils of everlasting suffering. They are quite different with regard to all other things. They are afraid of mere trifles; they foresee them; they feel them.

And this same man who spends so many days and nights in rage and despair for the loss of office, or for some imaginary insult to his honour, is the very one who knows without anxiety and without emotion that he will lose all by death. It is a monstrous thing to see in the same heart and at the same time this sensibility to trifles and this strange insensibility to the greatest objects. It is an incomprehensible enchantment, and a supernatural slumber, which indicates as its cause an all-powerful force. There must be a strange confusion in the nature of man, that he should boast of being in that state in which it seems incredible that a single individual should be.

However, experience has shown me so great a number of such persons that the fact would be surprising, if we did not know that the greater part of those who trouble themselves about the matter are disingenuous and not, in fact, what they say. They are people who have heard it said that it is the fashion to be thus daring. It is what they call "shaking off the yoke," and they try to imitate this. But it would not be difficult to make them understand how greatly they deceive themselves in thus seeking esteem. This is not the way to gain it, even I say among those men of the world who take a healthy view of things and who know that the only way to succeed in this life is to make ourselves appear honourable, faithful, judicious, and capable of useful service to a friend; because naturally men love only what may be useful to them.

Now, what do we gain by hearing it said of a man that he has now thrown off the yoke, that he does not believe there is a God who watches our actions, that he considers himself the sole master of his conduct, and that he thinks he is accountable for it only to himself? Does he think that he has thus brought us to have henceforth complete confidence in him and to look to him for consolation, advice, and help in every need of life? Do they profess to have delighted us by telling us that they hold our soul to be only a little wind and smoke, especially by telling us this in a haughty and self-satisfied tone of voice? Is this a thing to say gaily?

Is it not, on the contrary, a thing to say sadly, as the saddest thing in the world? If they thought of it seriously, they would see that this is so bad a mistake, so contrary to good sense, so opposed to decency, and so removed in every respect from that good breeding which they seek, that they would be more likely to correct than to pervert those who had an inclination to follow them. And, indeed, make them give an account of their opinions, and of the reasons which they have for doubting religion, and they will say to you things so feeble and so petty, that they persuade you of the contrary.

The following is what a person one day said to such a one very appositely: "If you continue to talk in this manner, you will really make me religious." And he was right, for who would not have a horror of holding opinions in which he would have such contemptible persons as companions! Thus those who only feign these opinions would be very unhappy, if they restrained their natural feelings in order to make themselves the most conceited of men. If, at the bottom of their heart, they are troubled at not having more light, let them not disguise the fact; this avowal will not be shameful. The only shame is to have none.

Nothing reveals more an extreme weakness of mind than not to know the misery of a godless man. Nothing is more indicative of a bad disposition of heart than not to desire the truth of eternal promises. Nothing is more dastardly than to act with bravado before God. Let them then leave these impieties to those who are sufficiently ill-bred to be really capable of them. Let them at least be honest men, if they cannot be Christians. Finally, let them recognise that there are two kinds of people one can call reasonable; those who serve God with all their heart because they know him, and those who seek him with all their heart because they do not know him. But as for those who live without knowing him and without seeking him, they judge themselves so little worthy of their own care, that they are not worthy of the care of others; and it needs all the charity of the religion which they despise, not to despise them even to the point of leaving them to their folly.

But because this religion obliges us always to regard them, so long as they are in this life, as capable of the grace which can enlighten them, and to believe that they may, in a little time, be more replenished with faith than we are, and that, on the other hand, we may fall into the blindness wherein they are, we must do for them what we would they should do for us if we were in their place, and call upon them to have pity upon themselves, and to take at least some steps in the endeavour to find light. Let them give to reading this some of the hours which they otherwise employ so uselessly; whatever aversion they may bring to the task, they will perhaps gain something, and at least will not lose much. But as for those who bring to the task perfect sincerity and a real desire to meet with truth, those I hope will be satisfied and convinced of the proofs of a religion so divine, which I have here collected, and in which I have followed somewhat after this order . . .

Before entering into the proofs of the Christian religion, I find it necessary to point out the sinfulness of those men who live in indifference to the search for truth in a matter which is so important to them, and which touches them so nearly. Of all their errors, this doubtless is the one which most convicts them of foolishness and blindness, and in which it is easiest to confound them by the first glimmerings of common sense and by natural feelings. For it is not to be doubted that the duration of this life is but a moment; that the state of death is eternal, whatever may be its nature; and that thus all our actions and thoughts must take such different directions, according to the state of that eternity, that it is impossible to take one step with sense and judgement, unless we regulate our course by the truth of that point which ought to be our ultimate end.

There is nothing clearer than this; and thus, according to the principles of reason, the conduct of men is wholly unreasonable, if they do not take another course. On this point, therefore, we condemn those who live without thought of the ultimate end of life, who let themselves be guided by their own inclinations and their own pleasures without reflection and without concern, and, as if they could annihilate eternity by turning away their thought from it, think only of making themselves happy for the moment.

Yet this eternity exists, and death, which must open into it and threatens them every hour, must in a little time infallibly put them under the dreadful necessity of being either annihilated or unhappy for ever, without knowing which of these eternities is for ever prepared for them. This is a doubt of terrible consequence. They are in peril of eternal woe and thereupon, as if the matter were not worth the trouble, they neglect to inquire whether this is one of those opinions which people receive with too credulous a facility, or one of those which, obscure in themselves, have a very firm, though hidden, foundation.

Thus they know not whether there be truth or falsity in the matter, nor whether there be strength or weakness in the proofs. They have them before their eyes; they refuse to look at them; and in that ignorance they choose all that is necessary to fall into this misfortune if it exists, to await death to make trial of it, yet to be very content in this state, to make profession of it, and indeed to boast of it. Can we think seriously of the importance of this subject without being horrified at conduct so extravagant? This resting in ignorance is a monstrous thing, and they who pass their life in it must be made to feel its extravagance and stupidity, by having it shown to them, so that they may be confounded by the sight of their folly. For this is how men reason, when they choose to live in such ignorance of what they are and without seeking enlightenment. "I know not," they say.

Endnotes

1   Michael D. O'Brien, talk at St. Patrick's Basilica in Ottawa, Canada, September 20, 2005, http://www.studiobrien.com/are-we-living-in-apocalyptic-times-part-1/.

2   Julian Baggini, *Atheism: A Very Short Introduction* (New York: Oxford University Press, 2003), 14.

3   Which implies, of course, that not all nontheists are indifferent absolutely, since some *do* take the arguments for theism seriously.

4   Deepak Chopra, *The Third Jesus: The Christ We Cannot Ignore* (New York: Harmony, 2008), 9-10.

5   John Henry Newman, *Essay on the Development of Doctrine* (Park Ridge: Word on Fire Publishing, 2017), 2.

6   For more technical definitions of these forms of indifferentism, see James Fox, "Religious Indifferentism," *The Catholic Encyclopedia*, vol. 7 (New York: Robert Appleton Company) retrieved May 17, 2016, http://www.newadvent.org/cathen/07759a.htm.

7   "Cardinal Ratzinger Calls Relativism 'Greatest Problem of Our Time," Zenit (September 26, 2003), https://zenit.org/articles/cardinal-ratzinger-calls-relativism-greatest-problem-of-our-time/.

8   Avery Dulles, *A History of Apologetics* (San Francisco: Ignatius Press, 2005), 166.

9   Blaise Pascal, *Pensées*, trans. A.J. Krailsheimer (New York: Penguin Classics, 1995), 4.

10 Ibid., 127-128.

11 Ibid., 130.

12 Ibid., 128.

13 G.K. Chesterton, *Collected Works*, vol. 1 (San Francisco: Ignatius Press, 1986), 217.

14 Ibid., 218.

15 Frank Sheed, *Knowing God: God and the Human Condition* (repr., San Francisco: Ignatius Press, 2012), 50.

16 Ibid., 51.

17 Ibid.

18 Frank Sheed, *Theology and Sanity* (repr., San Francisco: Ignatius Press, 1993), 7.

19 Here I am including the Eastern Orthodox churches under the "Catholic Church" umbrella, inasmuch as they have valid sacraments and authentic apostolic lineage.

20 Sheed, *Theology and Sanity*, 17.

21 Mother Teresa and Brian Kolodiejchuk, *Mother Teresa: Come Be My Light* (New York: Doubleday, 2007), 20.

22 Josef Ratzinger, *Introduction to Christianity*, rev. ed. (San Francisco: Ignatius Press, 2004), 46.

23 *Catechism of the Catholic Church*, 2125; Rom. 1:18.

24 Dwight Longenecker, "Blessed John Henry Newman Explains Faith Doubts and Difficulties," *National Catholic Register*, September 16, 2011.

25 G.K. Chesterton, *Collected Works*, vol. 1 (San Francisco: Ignatius Press, 1986), 318.

26 Robert Sokolowski, *Phenomenology of the Human Person* (Cambridge, England: Cambridge University Press, 2008), 21.

27 Augustine, *Confessions,* X, 23, 33.

28 Aristotle, *The Nicomachean Ethics*, eds. J.L. Ackrill and J.O. Urmson, trans. David Ross (New York: Oxford University Press, 2009), 5.

29 Pascal, *Pensées*, 123.

30 Thomas Merton, *The Seven Storey Mountain* (Park Ridge: Word on Fire Publishing), 15-16.

31 C.S. Lewis, *The Four Loves* (London: Harper Collins, 1998), 67.

32 Aristotle, *The Nicomachean Ethics*, 192.

33 *Jesus Christ the Bearer of the Water of Life*, 2.3.4.2, http://www.vatican.va/roman_curia/pontifical_councils/interelg/documents/rc_pc_interelg_doc_20030203_new-age_en.html.

34 "Living the Law of Attraction," Oprah.com, http://www.oprah.com/spirit/the-law-of-attraction-real-life-stories_1.

35 Credit goes to Edward Feser for this definition, which he provides in his *Philosophy of Mind* (London: Oneworld Publications, 2006).

36 Francis Crick, *The Astonishing Hypothesis: The Scientific Search for the Soul* (New York: Simon and Schuster, 1994), 3.

37 Natalie Thompson, "Law of Attraction in a Nutshell," *VibeShifting*, http://www.vibeshifting.com/law-of-attraction-in-a-nutshell/.

38 C.S. Lewis, *Mere Christianity* (New York: Harper Collins Publishing, 2001), 26.

39 David Hume, *An Inquiry Concerning Human Understanding*, I, 7.

40 Mitch Stokes, *How to Be an Atheist: Why Many Skeptics Aren't Skeptical Enough* (Wheaton, IL: Crossway, 2016), 42.

41 Alexander Rosenberg, *The Atheist's Guide to Reality: Enjoying Life Without Illusions* (New York: W.W. Norton, 2011), 2-3.

42 Anthony Cashmore, "The Lucretian Swerve: The Biological Basis of Human Behavior and the Criminal Justice System," *Proceedings of the National Academy of Sciences* 107, no. 10 (January 12, 2010):4499-4504.

43 Steven Weinberg, *The First Three Minutes: A Modern View of the Origin*

of the Universe (New York: Basic Books, 1993), 154.

44 William Lane Craig, *Reasonable Faith: Christian Truth and Apologetics*, 3rd ed. (Wheaton, IL: Crossway, 2008), 72.

45 J.R.R. Tolkien, *The Fellowship of the Ring* (London: Harper Collins Publishing, 2012), 67.

46 Ibid., 73.

47 Richard Lewontin, "Billions and Billions of Demons," *The New York Review of Books*, January 9, 1997, 31.

48 Bertrand Russell, *My Philosophical Development* (London: Unwin Paperbacks, 1985), 13.

49 G.K. Chesterton, *Collected Works*, vol. 1 (San Francisco: Ignatius Press, 1986), 225.

50 William Shakespeare, *Macbeth*, V, v, 20-31.

51 Thomas Nagel, *What Does It All Mean? A Very Short Introduction to Philosophy* (New York, Oxford University Press, 1987), 101.

52 Thomas Nagel, *Mind and Cosmos: Why the Materialist Neo-Darwinian Conception of Nature is Almost Certainly False* (New York: Oxford University Press, 2012), 123.

53 Ibid., 124; citing Francis Crick, *Life Itself: Its Origin and Nature* (New York: Simon & Schuster, 1982), 88.

54 Walter Stace, "Man Against Darkness," *Atlantic Monthly*, September 1948, in E.D. Klemke and Steven Cahn, eds., *The Meaning of Life: A Reader*, 3rd ed., (New York: Oxford University Press, 2007), 86.

55 Ibid., 86.

56 Ibid.

57 Ibid., 87.

58 David Oderberg, "Teleology: Inorganic or Organic," in A.M. Gonzalez, ed., *Contemporary Perspectives on Natural Law* (Aldershot, UK: Ashgate, 2008), 259.

59 Edward Feser, *Aquinas* (London: Oneworld Publications, 2017), 120.

60 Ibid., 115.

61 Jean-Paul Sartre, *Existentialism and Humanism*, trans. Philip Mairet (London: Methuen & Co., 1960), 28.

62 Edward Feser, *The Last Superstition: A Refutation of the New Atheism* (South Bend, IN: St. Augustine's Press, 2010), 221.

63 J.L. Mackie, *The Miracle of Theism* (New York: Oxford University Press, 1982), 115-116.

64 See also J.L. Mackie, *Ethics: Inventing Right and Wrong* (London: Penguin Books, 1990).

65 Jean Paul Sartre, "Existentialism is a Humanism," lecture at Club Maintenant in Paris, October 29, 1945.

66 Alexander Rosenberg, *The Atheist's Guide to Reality: Enjoying Life*

Without Illusions (New York: W.W. Norton, 2011), 3.

67   N.T. Wright, "Jesus and the Identity of God," *Ex Auditu* 14 (1998): 42–56.

68   Christians believe that God is three persons, distinct though not separate, who are co-equal, co-eternal, one in being.

69   Richard Dawkins, *The God Delusion* (London: Bantam Press, 2006), 101.

70   Ibid., 100.

71   For a robust defense of these arguments, I especially recommend Edward Feser, *Five Proofs for The Existence of God* (San Francisco: Ignatius Press, 2017).

72   David R. Allen, "God's Psychological Profile," richarddawkins.net, March 12, 2014, https://www.richarddawkins.net/2014/03/gods-psychological-profile/.

73   C.S. Lewis, *The Problem of Pain* (New York: Harper Collins Publishing, 1996), 3.

74   "Too Simple to be True," *Where All Roads Lead*, The Collected Works of G.K. Chesterton, Vol. 3 (San Francisco: Ignatius Press, 1990).

75   C.S. Lewis, *Surprised by Joy: The Shape of My Early Life* (London: Harper Collins Publishers, 2002), 133.

76   Lewis, *Mere Christianity*, 29.

77   Someone might object, "But what about Satan?" Satan was not *created* as evil; he was created good by God but, because of his own free choice, is now and forever corrupt.

78   C. Stephen Evans, *God and Moral Obligation* (New York: Oxford University Press, 2014), 62.

79   Martin Luther King Jr., "A Proper Sense of Priorities," speech given February 6, 1968, in Washington, DC.

80   Peter Kreeft, "The Argument from Conscience," in *Fundamentals of the Faith: Essays in Christian Apologetics* (San Francisco: Ignatius Press, 1988), 36–41.

81   John Henry Newman, "Letter to the Duke of Norfolk," V, in *Certain Difficulties felt by Anglicans in Catholic Teaching* II (London: Longmans Green, 1885), 248. Cf. *Catechism of the Catholic Church*, 1778.

82   Cited in Robert Spitzer, *The Soul's Upward Yearning: Clues to Our Transcendent Nature from Experience and Reason* (San Francisco: Ignatius Press, 2015), 73.

83   Kreeft, "The Argument from Conscience," 36–41.

84   John Henry Newman, *An Essay in Aid of a Grammar of Assent* (Notre Dame: University of Notre Dame Press, 2001), 101.

85   Lewis, *Mere Christianity*, 14.

86 John Henry Newman, Letter to J. Walker of Scarborough, May 22, 1868, *The Letters and Diaries of John Henry Newman* (Oxford: Clarendon Press, 1973).

87 Joseph Ratzinger, *In the Beginning: A Catholic Understanding of the Story of Creation and the Fall* (Grand Rapids: Eerdmans, 1995), 50.

88 Stokes, *How to Be an Atheist*, 174.

89 Ibid.

90 Marc Hauser and Peter Singer, "Morality Without Religion," *Free Inquiry* 26 (2005): 19.

91 Sam Harris, *The Moral Landscape: How Science Can Determine Human Values*, (New York: Free Press, 2010), 32.

92 Richard Taylor, *Ethics, Faith, and Reason* (Upper Saddle River, NJ: Prentice Hall, 1984), 9.

93 Ibid., 26.

94 G.K. Chesterton, *Collected Works*, vol. 1 (San Francisco: Ignatius Press, 1986), 217.

95 G.K. Chesterton, "Introduction to the Book of Job," https://www.chesterton.org/introduction-to-job/.

96 See Romans 1:20.

97 Pascal, *Pensées*, 150.

98 Peter Van Inwagen, "What Is the Problem of the Hiddenness of God?", in *Divine Hiddenness: New Essays*, eds. Daniel Howard-Snyder and Paul K. Moser (Cambridge, UK: Cambridge University Press, 2001), 31.

99 See James 2:19.

100 John Hick, *Evil and the God of Love* (New York: Harper and Row, 1977), 318-336.

101 Michael Murray, "Deus Absconditus," in *Divine Hiddenness: New Essays*, eds. Daniel Howard-Snyder and Paul K. Moser (New York: Cambridge University Press, 2002), 65.

102 Pascal, *Pensées*, 72.

103 Peter Kreeft, *Summa of the Summa: The Essential Philosophical Passages of the Summa Theologica* (San Francisco: Ignatius Press, 1990), 101.

104 Travis Dumsday, "C.S. Lewis on the Problem of Divine Hiddenness," *The Anglican Theological Review* (Winter 2015): 45.

105 Ibid., 42.

106 "The Question of God: An Interview with Francis Collins," PBS.org, 2004, http://www.pbs.org/wgbh/questionofgod/voices/collins.html.

107 Ibid.

108 William Rowe, "The Problem of Evil and Some Varieties of Atheism," *American Philosophical Quarterly* 16 (October 1979): 335.

109 William Lane Craig, *On Guard: Defending Your Faith with Reason and*

Precision (Colorado Springs: David C. Cook, 2010), 158-161.

110 Herbert McCabe, *God Matters* (London: Mowbray, 2000), 45.

111 Christopher Dawson, "The Christian View of History," *New Blackfriars* 32 (July 1951): 312-27.

112 Paul Rhodes Eddy and Gregory Boyd, *The Jesus Legend: A Case for the Historical Reliability of the Synoptic Jesus Tradition* (Ada, MI: Baker Academic, 2007), 143.

113 Ibid.

114 N.T. Wright, *The Resurrection of the Son of God* (Minneapolis: Fortress Press, 2003), 80.

115 Ibid., 82.

116 Bart Ehrman, *Did Jesus Exist?: The Historical Argument for Jesus of Nazareth* (New York: HarperOne, 2012), 230.

117 Bruce Metzger, "Considerations of Methodology in the Study of the Mystery Religions and Early Christianity," *Harvard Theological Review* 48, no. 1 (January 1955): 1-20.

118 Martin Hengel, *The Son of God: The Origin of Christology and the History of Jewish-Hellenistic Religion*, trans. J. Bowden (Philadelphia: Fortress, 1976), 27.

119 See Gary Michuta's *Hostile Witnesses* (El Cajon, CA: Catholic Answers Press, 2017).

120 Ehrman, *Did Jesus Exist?*, 4.

121 N.T. Wright, as quoted in Antony Flew and Roy Abraham Varghese, *There Is A God* (New York: Harper Collins Publishers, 2008), 187.

122 As quoted in Eddy and Boyd, *The Jesus Legend*, 166.

123 Josephus, *Antiquities of the Jews,* 20.9.1.

124 Eddy and Boyd, *The Jesus Legend*, 190.

125 *Antiquities* 18.3.3.

126 Eddy and Boyd, *The Jesus Legend*, 199.

127 Tacitus, *Annals* 15.44. Translation from Latin by A. J. Church and W. J. Brodribb, 1876.

128 For the following, see Eddy and Boyd, *The Jesus Legend*, 168.

129 John Meier, *A Marginal Jew: Rethinking the Historical Jesus,* vol. 1 (New Haven: Yale University Press, 1991), 56.

130 From Leo Baker, "Near the Beginning," in *Remembering C.S. Lewis: Recollections of Those Who Knew Him*, ed. James Como (San Francisco: Ignatius Press, 2005).

131 Lewis, *Surprised by Joy*, 63.

132 This is not to say that there aren't miracles attributed to the other religious figures. Although Buddha and Muhammad have had miracles attributed to them, the evidence for them is negligible compared to that for the miracles of Christ.

133 Michael Buckley, S.J., *At the Origins of Modern Atheism* (New Haven: Yale University Press, 1990), 40.

134 Lewis, *Mere Christianity*, 52.

135 Brant Pitre, *The Case for Jesus: The Biblical and Historical Evidence for Christ* (New York: Image Books, 2016).

136 Ibid., 80-82.

137 Graham Stanton, foreword to Richard Burridge, *What Are The Gospels?: A Comparison with Graeco-Roman Biography* (Grand Rapids, MI: Eerdmans, 2004), xi.

138 Pope Benedict XVI, *Jesus of Nazareth: The Infancy Narratives*, trans. Philip J. Whitmore (New York: Random House Large Print, 2012), 29.

139 Pitre, *Case for Jesus*, 76.

140 Pitre, *Case for Jesus*, 23.

141 Trent Horn, *Hard Sayings: A Catholic Approach to Answering Bible Difficulties* (El Cajon, CA: Catholic Answers Press, 2016), 340-341.

142 Craig Blomberg, *Can We Still Believe in the Bible?: An Evangelical Engagement With Contemporary Questions* (Ada, MI: Brazos Press, 2014), 27-28.

143 Bart Ehrman, *Misquoting Jesus* (New York: HarperSanFrancisco, 2005), 252-253.

144 Augustine, *Contra Faustum*, 11.5.

145 Craig Blomberg, *The Historical Reliability of the Gospels* (Downers Grove, IL: IVP Academic, 2007), 53.

146 Curtis Mitch and Scott Hahn, *Ignatius Catholic Study Bible: New Testament* (San Francisco: Ignatius Press, 2010), 201.

147 Richard Bauckham, *Jesus and the Eyewitnesses: The Gospels as Eyewitness Testimony* (Grand Rapids: Eerdmans, 2017), 124.

148 Ibid., 346.

149 This has been lost, but parts have been preserved in Origen's rebuttal, *Against Celsus*.

150 Eddy and Boyd, *The Jesus Legend*, 178.

151 Rabbi Jacob Neusner, as quoted in Pope Benedict XVI, *Jesus of Nazareth: From the Baptism in the Jordan to the Transfiguration*, trans. Adrian J. Walker. (New York: Doubleday, 2007), 115.

152 Gary Habermas, "The Minimal Facts Approach to the Resurrection of Jesus: The Role of Methodology as a Crucial Component in Establishing Historicity," *Southeastern Theological Review* 3, no.1 (Summer 2012): 15–26, http://www.garyhabermas.com/articles/southeastern_theological_review/minimal-facts-methodology_08-02-2012.htm.

153 See John Dominic Crossan, *Jesus: A Revolutionary Biography* (San Francisco: HarperOne, 2009), 145, 154, 196, 201.

154 The Gospels represent at least two independent sources of eyewitness attestation, the synoptic Gospels collectively and John.

155 G.K. Chesterton, *Collected Works I*, 343.

156 Michael Licona, *The Resurrection of Jesus: A New Historiographical Approach* (Downers Grove, IL: IVP Academic, 2010), 306.

157 James D.G. Dunn, *Jesus Remembered* (Grand Rapids: Eerdmans, 2003), 855.

158 Josephus, *Antiquities*, 18.63-64.

159 Tacitus, *Annals*, 15.44.

160 William Edwards, Wesley Gabel, and Floyd Hosmer, "On the Physical Death of Jesus Christ," *JAMA* 255, no. 11 (March 21, 1986):1455-1463.

161 Craig Keener, *Miracles: The Credibility of the New Testament Accounts* (Ada, MI: Baker Academic, 2011).

162 Interview in "The Search for Jesus with Peter Jennings," ABC News (June 26, 2000), as quoted in Habermas, *The Minimal Facts Approach*.

163 N.T. Wright, "The New, Unimproved Jesus," *Christianity Today*, September 13, 1993, 26.

164 See Acts 9; Gal. 1:13; 1 Cor. 9:1.

165 N.T. Wright defends this brilliantly in *The Resurrection of the Son of God*, Christian Origins and the Question of God, vol. 3 (Minneapolis: Fortress Press, 2016).

166 See Rom. 12; 1 Cor. 12; and Col. 1.

167 See also CCC 795.

168 Bret Stetka, "Extended Adolescence: When 25 Is the New 18," *Scientific American*, September 19, 2017, https://www.scientificamerican. com/article/extended-adolescence-when-25-is-the-new-181/.

169 Steve Weidenkopf, "Reformation: Myths & Revolution," February 22, 2015, http://soul-candy.info/2015/02/reformation-myths-revolution/.

170 Hilaire Belloc, *Characters of the Reformation* (San Francisco: Ignatius Press, 2017), 17.

171 Augustine, *Sermons to Catechumens on the Creed*, 7:15.

172 Robert Barron, foreword to John Henry Newman, *An Essay on the Development of Christian Doctrine* (Des Plaines, IL: Word on Fire, 2017).

173 Justin Martyr, *First Apology*, 65.

174 Ibid., 66.

175 Marcus Grodi, "The Early Church Fathers I Never Saw," Coming Home Network International, April 24, 2012, https://chnetwork. org/2012/04/24/the-early-church-fathers-i-never-saw-by-marcus-grodi/.

176 Ignatius of Antioch, Letter to the Smyrnaeans, 8.

177 Ibid., 6.1.

178 Clement, Letter to the Corinthians, 42:4–5, 44:1–3.

179 G.K. Chesterton, "The Language of Eternity," *The Illustrated London News*, July 2, 1910.

180 See also Matt. 18:18.

181 See Irenaeus, *Against Heresies*, 3.3.3.

182 Cyprian, *The Unity of the Catholic Church*, 4.

183 Jimmy Akin, "A Triumph and a Tragedy," in *Surprised by Truth: 11 Converts Give the Biblical and Historical Reasons for Being Catholic,* ed. Patrick Madrid, (Basilica Press, 1994).

184 Tertullian, *Baptism*, 1.

185 Cyprian, *The Lapsed*, 15:28.

186 Aidan Nichols, *Christendom Awake: On Reenergizing the Church in Culture* (Grand Rapids: Eerdmans, 1999), 21.

187 "Carl Lentz to Oprah: 'That's Why Jesus Came, So You Didn't Need a Priest in the Middle,'" October 14, 2016, http://www.supersoul.tv/supersoul-full-episodes/pastor-carl-lentz-full-episode.

188 Scott Hahn, "Hunt for the Fourth Cup," *Catholic Answers* magazine, September 1, 1991.

189 Malachi 1:11.

190 *Didache* 14.

191 Clement, *Miscellanies*, 6:13:107:2.

192 Humphrey Carpenter, ed., *The Letters of J.R.R. Tolkien* (New York: Mariner Books, 2000), 53.

193 Peter Kreeft, *Before I Go: Letters to Our Children about What Really Matters* (Lanham, MD: Sheed & Ward, 2007), 51.

194 Augustine, *Holy Virginity*, 6:6.

195 Irenaeus, *Against Heresies*, 3:22:24.

196 Ephraim, *Nisibene Hymns*, 27:8.

197 Martin Luther, "On the Day of the Conception of the Mother of God," 1527.

198 Ambrose, *The Virgins*.

199 Leslie Rumble, *Radio Replies* (San Diego: Catholic Answers, 2014), 11.

200 Michael Lipka, "A closer look at America's rapidly growing religious 'nones'," Facttank, http://www.pewresearch.org/fact-tank/2015/05/13/a-closer-look-at-americas-rapidly-growing-religious-nones/.

201 Peter Kreeft, ed., *Christianity for Modern Pagans: Pascal's Pensées* (San Francisco: Ignatius Press, 1993), 4.

202 John Paul II, *Fides et Ratio,* September 14, 1998. http://w2.vatican.va/content/john-paul-ii/en/encyclicals/documents/hf_jp-ii_enc_14091998_fides-et-ratio.html.

203 Alexandr Solzhenitsyn, Nobel Lecture in Literature (1970), https://www.nobelprize.org/nobel_prizes/literature/laureates/1970/solzhenitsyn-lecture.html.

204 Jean-Baptiste Chautard, *The Soul of the Apostolate* (Charlotte: TAN Books, 2010), 161.

205 Robert Barron, *The Priority of Christ: Toward a Postliberal Catholicism* (Grand Rapids: Baker Academic, 2016), 342.

206 http://www.ntslibrary.com/PDF%20Books/Blaise%20Pascal%20 Pensees.pdf, 194-195.

About the Author

Matthew Nelson obtained his bachelor's degree in physical education from the University of Regina, and his doctor of chiropractic from the Canadian Memorial Chiropractic College in Toronto. He resides in Shaunavon, Canada, with his wife and two daughters. You can follow Matt at his blog, ReasonableCatholic.com.